PAUL VITALE

# SELL WITH CONFIDENCE

## UNLOCK YOUR POTENTIAL

Published by Vital Communications, Inc.
Post Office Box 2042
Little Rock, Arkansas 72203

Vital Communications, Inc. titles may be purchased in bulk for educational, business, fund-raising or sales promotional use. For information, please call 501-868-8195.

Library of Congress Control Number 2009920559

ISBN 978-0-9666174-4-3

First Edition

Cover Design
Chuck Robertson

Cover Photo
Keith Saveall

Internal Design & Typesetting
Pam Bozeman

Proofreader
Debra Villiger

This publication is designed to provide accurate and authoritative information with regard to the subject matter covered. It is sold with the understanding that the publisher is not engaged in rendering legal, accounting or other professional advice. If legal advice or other expert assistance is required, the services of a competent professional person should be sought.

— From a *Declaration of Principles* jointly adopted by a Committee of the American Bar Association and a Committee of Publishers and Associations

Printed in the United States of America

*To my wife, Jessica; my parents, Lou and Carole; my brother, Matt.*
*Thank you for your unwavering support.*

# A Special Thanks

You are only as good as the people you're surrounded by. To Pam Bozeman for your unending contribution to the content, internal design and typesetting of this book—I commend you for a job well done. To Chuck Robertson and Keith Saveall for your creativity and attention to detail with the front cover; to Debra Villiger, Ellen Hart, Scott Hardin, Trace Thurlby and Maggie Milligan for your assistance during the final stages of this project; and to you, the reader—thank you for trusting in the knowledge found on the following pages.

# TABLE OF CONTENTS

The seed of potential is planted in each of us. The direction it grows and for how long is up to you.

~ Paul Vitale

# INTRODUCTION

Walk into any bookstore and you will find dozens of books and numerous resources teaching the magic formulas of salesmanship. Many of the concepts outlined will help; however, unless you first have confidence in yourself and in the product and/or service you represent, your success rate will be greatly limited.

Your first impression on others, either in person or over the telephone, greatly influences the outcome. The door will either swing open or stay closed depending on how well you relate to your potential clientele. To this end, you will benefit by presenting yourself in such a way that you are deserving of the client's business, and then represent your product or service with the same zest and commitment.

Are you making the most out of every sales opportunity? Do you write your own script for success, or do you allow circumstances to steer your course? Do you follow through impeccably well? To master the skills of salesmanship, questions such as these and many others should be analyzed quite frequently.

I'm of the opinion that to unlock your full potential, you must pause for a moment and pay close attention to your own sales process. The time spent in reflection is an investment in your future with a guaranteed return of self-improvement.

**Do I honestly believe in what I am selling?** You must have a passion to sell your product or service. If you are not passionate about what you are selling, people will recognize this and become skeptical. Expressing true passion and a deep belief will definitely help set you apart from the competition. When you are able to persuade people to believe in your product or service as much as you do, you will not only make the sale, you will make a difference.

**Do I really understand the product or service I stand behind?** It is extremely noticeable to your clients when you don't understand the nuts and bolts of what you are trying to promote. You might slide by for a while, but sooner or later your knowledge and understanding will be tested. It's important to realize that your name and reputation are attached to your product or service. In today's competitive business climate, it is much easier to initially learn as much as possible about what you represent than to try to regain the trust of your clients after a product or service has failed their expectations.

**Is providing quality customer service a part of my regimen?** Regardless of your job title, position in an organization or experience, your number one task will always be to attract, satisfy and preserve customers. It is essential to keep in mind that customer satisfaction, retention and loyalty are achieved by exceeding what clients anticipate in positive ways. Exceeding customers' expectations on a consistent basis pays major dividends at the end of the day.

**Am I capable of handling rejection?** There is one guarantee in sales: You might be passionate and well-versed about your product or service, but rejection is going to take place. Remember, every "no" is one no closer to a "yes." Learn to accept rejection, remove it from your mind and then move forward. No one enjoys being rejected; still, if you improve from it, you and your business will be strengthened.

Being provided with the opportunity to educate others on what you offer can be as enjoyable or as miserable as you make it. Either way, you are in control of your environment, technique and attitude. If you truly want the door to open, you must believe it will and persist until it does.

SELL WITH CONFIDENCE — UNLOCK YOUR POTENTIAL has been written with you in mind: the sales professional who strives to build quality business relationships, assist clients, deliver positive results and stand behind what's delivered.

As you approach each of this book's independent chapters, be prepared to examine concepts such as the human factor of selling as well as the entire process of salesmanship—from start to finish. Being enthusiastic about your product or service generates a passion for the people who consume it and, in the end, isn't that what salesmanship is all about? People!

As a salesperson, you must be committed to achieving your utmost potential, even when the going gets tough. The opportunity of reaching full stride hinges on a number of variables. Successful sales representatives have discovered the art of representing their products or services in such a way that positive results are inevitable. Earning the opportunity to build your business, one client at a time, takes a steady plan that is grounded in proven techniques—not here today, gone tomorrow practices. Count on thoroughly exploring these concepts in the chapters ahead.

Following the final chapter, you'll find several valuable sections including *Answers to Fifteen Essential Questions*, *Thirteen Habits of Pitching With Confidence* and *Twenty Tips to Providing Quality Customer Care*. These featured sections will assist you as you strive to sharpen your presentation skills and consistently exceed your customers' expectations.

It is my sincere hope that you find what you are searching for, not only as a successful representative of your product or service, but also as an individual who has the privilege of assisting people with their needs and wants each and every day. My wish is that **SELL WITH CONFIDENCE — UNLOCK YOUR POTENTIAL** will lend a hand as you continue journeying toward unlocking your full potential as an effective ambassador. I encourage you to take away the knowledge found in this book and apply it as often as possible. Granted, some days will always be tougher than others, but keep this in mind: It takes a special person to do what you do. For this, I commend you!

All the best,

**PAUL VITALE**
Little Rock, Arkansas

# SELL WITH CONFIDENCE

## UNLOCK YOUR POTENTIAL

# 1

# COMMIT TO REACHING YOUR FULL POTENTIAL

"What lies behind us and what lies before us are tiny matters compared to what lies within us." I can't help but wonder if Ralph Waldo Emerson, when penning this short quotation, wasn't shining a bright light on the importance of self-confidence. I have often been reminded: My background and circumstances may have influenced who I am, but I am responsible for who I become. Having self-confidence is not about being arrogant, but possessing a true belief in the ability to succeed. In business, this is never as important as when promoting a product or service.

More often than not, you may find that being committed to reaching your full potential begins with the answer to this one simple question: Where does my self-confidence measure today?

There are frequent reminders that life's battles don't discriminate. However, the choice to let circumstances control your mind-set lies within. If you think you have been beaten, you definitely have; if you would like to achieve, but think you can't, it is almost certain you won't; if your self-confidence is lost, so is the passion that moves you.

Possessing a strong self-belief is the keystone for unsurpassed achievement. Without a doubt, inner confidence affects outer results. To be truly effective in sales, I have come to the overwhelming conclusion that it unquestionably begins from the inside out.

To that point, you must not only have a true understanding of your product or service, but it is essential that you be passionate about what you are representing. When knowledge coupled with passion is present, successful results are abundant. For instance, let's consider this hypothetical situation: You have just accepted a position as an account executive for a leading soft drink company and are responsible for various in-store promotions at locations throughout the Northeast. Although you seldom consume soft drinks, you honestly believe you can promote and sell the leading beverage your company produces. Week after week, you arrive at locations setting up displays, answering questions from vendors, and mixing and mingling with loyal customers. Many of the questions you are asked center on logistics. "When can we expect our weekly shipment?" "How long should the current display stay standing?" "When will the new accounting system be implemented at the corporate office?"

On the other hand, mixed in with these questions are inquiries about the drink itself. "Do you enjoy this soda as much as I do?" "Which do you like better, regular or diet?" "How many cases do you and your family go through in a week?" It's not until you begin receiving these types of questions that your overall knowledge is challenged and your self-confidence is affected.

To be passionate about something, you must buy in—hook, line and sinker. In this particular scenario, it is important to be able to personally speak from experience. The logistical questions require specific answers.

The questions of a personal nature require firsthand knowledge and your formed opinion—background that not only comes from using the product, but being excited about it and truly enjoying it.

Across the board, some of the most successful sales representatives do more than just promote their causes, they make them a part of their everyday lives. When individuals truly commit to a personal or professional undertaking, it permeates everything they do, becoming part of who they are. Just as self-confidence, knowledge and passion assist you in reaching your full potential, let's consider how your state of mind is a crucial factor as well.

## _It truly is a state of mind_

Have you ever wondered what the unmistakable differences are between those who thrive in selling their products or services and those who often struggle? Is there a certain state of mind that seems to be consistently linked with achievement, or does the approach taken when communicating with a prospect really even matter?

On a number of different occasions, I have had the opportunity to observe individuals introduce their products or services in many different ways. Approaches and product knowledge have varied. For those who make a habit of being successful, one characteristic is never absent: the right mental attitude.

Throughout your life, you have no doubt listened to others explain the benefits of optimism versus pessimism. Some bought into the idea of viewing the glass half-full rather than half-empty, while others have disregarded such a thought. Nonetheless, when provided the opportunity to promote, sell or service what you represent, shouldn't a positive outlook be part of the approach? There is no question it's crucial to be well-informed about what you stand behind, but at the same time you must be aware of your mind-set.

The third President of the United States, Thomas Jefferson, once remarked, "Nothing can stop the man with the right mental attitude from achieving his goal; nothing on earth can help the man with the wrong attitude." To reach your full potential, it behooves you to commit to a mind-set of competence, benevolence, eagerness and honesty. These attributes, along with others, have a direct effect on the people you come into contact with, either over the telephone or in person.

*Skills of a Successful Sales Representative*

❖ Exercises enthusiasm
❖ Demonstrates a positive attitude
❖ Self-disciplined
❖ Sets obtainable goals
❖ Extensive product knowledge
❖ Good prospecting
❖ Possesses self-confidence
❖ Qualifies clients
❖ Dynamic presenter
❖ Handles objections
❖ Obtains quality introductions
❖ Closes the sale

There will always be those days when you would rather not be optimistic about what you are promoting, instances when the energy level in your battery pack is low. On days such as these it is definitely "gut check" time, the moment you have to reach deep inside and pull yourself up by your bootstraps. When setting the course for your attitude, the direction you follow will steer you either to a place of fulfillment or dissatisfaction.

What causes moments like these? What can be done to improve your state of mind? When you are neither yourself nor performing at the level you are accustomed to, it's imperative to stop and take a hard look at the reasons why. Through this type of self-assessment, the answers you discover will help you see things from a different point of view.

For instance, I have found when my tolerance level is being tested to the max and my outlook is not the most pleasant, I can usually link the cause back to various factors, one being the lack of quality rest. As a professional, it is pertinent to get the sleep you need to perform at the level you expect daily. Understanding how some circumstances and situations can prevent this, it should still be a viable goal. I think you would agree it's quite taxing to walk around in a fog the day after being deprived of much-needed sleep the night before. It is one thing to be physically present, but if your body and mind are completely worn out, being mentally alert can become a huge chore.

Another condition that has derailed my own state of mind is not being completely prepared. Preparation has an extremely large influence on my confidence level and, in turn, my way of thinking. If I have taken ample time to prepare, by and large my mind-set is where it needs to be. Then again, if I have waited until the last minute, my position changes. I believe it is a safe bet to say we all procrastinate occasionally. When this happens, think about the level of stress you experience. Does it have a positive or negative effect on your outlook? Is your confidence level jeopardized by anxiety and, as a result, does your approach suffer?

These types of revealing questions are worth asking to help you not only recognize the causes, but to also help you discover useful solutions. Self-evaluation is crucial to fighting back during the low points and has a great deal to do with your next necessary skill, the ability to handle objections.

## Handling objections

Many years ago while attending a sales training, the subject of handling objections came up. One of the participants in the class shared a unique angle that has helped me countless times to put the idea of rejection into perspective.

Joe suggested we all take out a pen and make a list of the most common objections our clients have ever had regarding our products or services. Next, he asked us to classify each opposition into one of two categories—a liability or a misunderstanding. In this case, a liability would be something that simply could not be provided.

For example, let's say you are a sales representative for a local furniture store. A patron walks in and would like to buy a particular brand of recliner that your store doesn't carry. This is a liability—something that prevents a successful outcome. On the flip side, let's assume that you carry the brand but the customer is ready to go to a competitor because of a clearance sale, unaware you might be able to match the price. This is a classic example of a misunderstanding—something you can provide that the client perceives you can't.

After constructing the list, Joe suggested that we each compare how many objections were labeled a liability versus a misunderstanding. Once I did this, I was pleasantly surprised with the results. Most of the protests I had dealt with in the past were not liabilities, they were simple misunderstandings. Since that was the case, I felt if I could do a better job of educating my clientele on the specifics of what I offer, I would become that much more successful, while identifying with the cause of the initial hesitation. To accomplish this, though, I had to not only be the one to speak, but more importantly the one to listen. Valuable wisdom is always gained when you receive feedback from your customers. Salespeople produce greater results when uncovering the reasons why patrons are resistant in the first place. What can make the product or service more effective? How can the delivery process be improved? Is the support staff living up to the customer's expectations? Is the service department customer-friendly? Skillfully handling customer opposition enables sales professionals to bounce back after a negative client response.

Handling clients' objections and rebounding from rejection will always have to be dealt with in the area of sales. In any case, try not to take others' resistance personally and become defensive. Remember you are not alone: It has been noted that the thought of being turned down tops the list of fears by many—the worry of not making it through the front door, let alone closing the sale if you do. Manage each situation the best you can despite the outcome, continuing to build relationships based on honesty, integrity and trust. If you do this, the odds of future success are excellent. It's this type of forward thinking that will enable you to persevere in the face of the many difficulties and setbacks you encounter as you get up, brush yourself off and finish what you started.

## Finish what you start

Committing to reach your full potential does indeed call for a strong mind-set accompanied by the ability to handle opposition. Also called to the forefront is the dedication to finish what you set out to accomplish in the first place.

Recall the last time you made a pledge to yourself or anyone else to begin a project and see it through to completion. How did it feel when your plans came together and you finished the task? Were you satisfied with the process or were there numerous variables that caused you grief? Did you complete the job in a timely manner, or was an extension needed? Aside from the answers to any of these questions, one fact rings true—you finished! That's right, regardless of all the hills and valleys traveled, at the end of the day you accomplished what you set out to achieve. Can anything be more satisfying?

Finishing what you start, whether on a grand scale or one of modest proportion, can be an extremely gratifying feeling. When your actions of honesty, integrity and trust culminate in new business, when you follow through on a promise to a customer and an expectation is exceeded, when you are asked to deliver an important presentation on behalf of the company and your countless hours of preparation pay off, the feeling of accomplishment will carry over into your next endeavor. These few examples illustrate the return on the investment received when you make the choice to complete the tasks you set out to achieve.

Be aware that the same momentum felt when realizing your accomplishments can spin off in a counterproductive direction as well. We all know individuals who have had good intentions, but they stop there. "I meant to return Mr. Johnson's call, but the day just flew by." "I assumed Sharon was putting all the presentation slides together, and now it is too late." "I had planned to back up my computer files, just in case something like this ever happened." If you've heard these types of statements once, you have heard them a thousand times.

Having good intentions is where you begin. Your point of difference comes in finding the motivation to leap over the hurdles of excuses. Naturally, there will always be honest explanations and justifications for not completing an assignment; nevertheless, to get from one end to the other, it is best to run past the reasons that might otherwise slow you down. When you are able to do this, completing tasks consistently will become second nature and you will be poised to reach your maximum potential. Don't ever forget the pure delight you felt the first time you achieved something you never believed would happen. Let that feeling carry you through to the finish line each and every time you commit to finishing what you start.

Each of the three major concepts presented within this chapter revolves around you looking inward. No matter the product or service, it is you who ignites the excitement, thoughts and perceptions surrounding what and/or who you represent. From having self-confidence, knowledge and passion, to an attitude that handles rejection well, committing to reach your full potential is a conscious choice only you can make. It is good to be reminded often: It is not a sprint you are running, but a marathon. This simple thought will go a long way as you continue developing your tenacious spirit.

## ∽⌒ CALL TO ACTION ⌒∼

Rest is the basis for a solid performance. Commit to going to bed one hour earlier than usual three of the next five nights. See if you can tell the difference in your daily approach and productivity.

When preparing a pitch for a client, instead of waiting until the eleventh hour, gather your thoughts and lay out your plan at least two days before your meeting. See if this affects your confidence level.

9

Experience rejection? Revisit one account that was lost in the past. Today, pick up the telephone, write a note or send an e-mail—touch base with the lost account. See if you can rekindle the flame.

# 2

# STRUCTURE THE DAY TO WORK IN YOUR FAVOR

In the rapid pace of a typical day, it is quite easy to become inundated by piles of paper, countless e-mails and annoying clutter. When the many mounds of responsibility call you to duty, remaining organized is extremely important to a successful outcome.

Individuals who make a conscious effort to establish an effective system which consistently works for them are normally able to stay on track—versus becoming derailed. You might start over the weekend, the night before or the early morning of, but taking time to get yourself and your space organized pays large dividends.

This theory applies to a variety of areas that makes up both your routine and mind-set. It also has an astonishing effect on the level of productivity reached on a daily basis.

Now, some might take issue with the idea that those who are better organized accomplish more tasks than those who aren't, but studies have shown that if you want to accomplish more in less time—you must organize your work space and yourself.

Whether you work in a corporate office, in a home office or out of your car, the lack of a sound structure costs you more than you may think. It drains your time, zaps your energy and prevents you from reaching your full potential—let alone the negative effect on your bottom line.

According to *The Wall Street Journal*®, the typical sales executive loses up to six weeks per year retrieving misplaced information from cluttered desks and files. On top of that, studies have found that Americans waste nine million hours per day searching for misplaced items. It has been said that organizational competence is not a matter of instinct, but of education and habit.

With that said, let's focus on how you can structure the day to work in your favor.

## *Your mental routine*

As previously stated, the right mental attitude is critical to a successful outcome as a sales representative. It is no different when it comes to having the right mental routine. Yes, it is important that quality rest becomes a part of your regimen and that sound preparation is never underestimated. There are a few other components of your mental routine that are worth recognizing as well in order to accomplish the desired results. The following are five simple questions that need to be answered frequently to maintain organization:

**What am I focused on today?** It is extremely difficult at times to concentrate your effort or attention on one particular thing. In a society where multi-tasking is expected, losing sight of the goal at hand is an easy thing to do. Much like a juggler, I also try to perfect the talent of having many balls in the air at once. I often find the entire process quite challenging.

Whether you must stop sometimes and just breathe, or combine the three separate sticky notes you have your "to-do" lists scribbled on, do your best to focus. Give proper attention to what needs to be done and then move on to the next task. I realize this might be more difficult than it sounds, but once you become adept at focusing you will recognize when it is time to slow down and reorganize your thoughts.

**What distractions continuously keep me from being productive?** Distractions often happen at the most inopportune times. When something interferes with your concentration and draws attention away from the task at hand, your productivity suffers. In the world of sales, numerous distractions are lurking around any corner. From your iPhone ringing during an important client meeting, to a colleague's voice reverberating from the adjacent cubicle, interruptions will always find a way to sneak into your daily routine. Recognize this, and do your best to either prepare for or eliminate as many of these disruptions as possible. When you are able to implement a steady workflow with consistency, the results are positive.

**Are my verbal and non-verbal reactions respectful to others?** It holds true that it's not what you say, it's how you say it that really matters. Allow this thought to prompt you to take note of how you come across to others in both verbal and non-verbal responses. From time to time, I illustrate this point with the help of a tube of toothpaste. If you remove the cap from a tube of toothpaste, squeeze a small portion into your hand and then attempt to put the toothpaste back in the tube, it can get pretty messy. The tube of toothpaste is no different than your mouth. Once you squeeze the words out, they have been spoken. Even if you wanted to put them back in, it's impossible to do. You might clarify, explain, apologize or try to correct the statements, but in the process, things can become quite muddled. This concept holds true to your non-verbal reactions as well—actions leave memorable impressions long after you have gone.

**Do I give an honest day's work through being punctual and timely?** One of the greatest pet peeves of those responsible for the bottom line is when an individual uses the clock dishonestly. On any given day, there are multiple ways of eating up time in an unproductive manner.

I can remember when I was in outside sales how tempting it was to take advantage of the freedom of time: whether not starting right at eight o'clock, stretching out the lunch hour, running personal errands on company time or finishing the day just a bit early. The lure was there, but I found myself thinking, "Am I giving an honest day's work to the firm?" This turned out to be a valuable question that not only served me well then, but also when I had my first opportunity to take a management position. I was often in conversations with my staff about the importance of being punctual—usually as it pertained to arriving at work on time and being fair with the lunch hour. Not too far behind that was the discussion about why it is important to be on time to meetings, receptions and anywhere else the business was represented. It makes no difference what position I have ever held, I've always thought this point boils down to respect—having respect for your client's time, the management who enforces the rules and your fellow colleagues who watch you execute your daily routine.

**Am I truly motivated to continue representing my product or service?** If you are motivated to represent the product or service you sell, the answers to the previous four questions should come quite easily. Let me reiterate, there will be times when it would be much easier to roll over and give up, or perhaps just simply not show up.

Self-starting effective sales representatives are not only extremely organized when it comes to their mental routine, they know what they

14

expect and are eager to share with others what can be expected of them. These individuals take great pride not only in what they are promoting, but how they promote it. Their focus is as pinpointed as a laser beam of light on the target they have in their sights. When they begin their day, they are motivated, and when they end their day, they remain excited about what they represent. Very few things knock them off stride or disrupt the passion that comes from within. Motivation is what moves them from good to great.

## *Your physical routine*

Just as important as your mental routine is your physical routine. Your dietary, exercise and stress management habits can keep you lethargic or transform you into a bundle of energy, ready to conquer the world of sales. Physical fitness can be critical to personal and professional success; make certain to recognize how your personal fitness habits affect your productivity.

15

If you spend a great deal of your day behind the wheel of your vehicle or sitting at your desk making telephone calls, make it a point to stop periodically, stretch your legs and take a brisk walk. Keep healthy snacks on hand, and make every attempt to avoid stress eating.

To be at your physical best, structure a fitness routine that you are comfortable with and then make time to follow it through. Whether you travel extensively or never leave your home base, exercise should be a part of each day's activities. If you smoke, cut back on your usage or, better yet, consider quitting. Use alcohol in moderation and if you attend frequent socials to mingle with clients, get in the habit of drinking soft drinks or sparkling water. A clear head will serve you well when networking and trying to establish and maintain long-lasting relationships.

Too often ignored, stress management is a vital skill to acquire when working in sales. Let's face it: Sales is a high-energy, high-stress, high-demand career. You learn how to talk on the telephone, network, ask questions, overcome objections and close the deal—but seldom are you taught how to cope with the chaos. Stress alone will zap your energy, but the end result is a condition no one wants to endure: burnout. By finding ways to handle your job-related stress, the chances for encountering burnout will diminish.

Take five when you're feeling particularly overwhelmed. Listen to some soothing music, or just find a quiet place and silence all telephones and pagers. Breathe deeply and clear your mind. Concentrate on something that is pleasing to you. If things have been building and you need a day or two off, allow yourself this time to recoup your energy. Look for ways to incorporate time to decompress every day, and find activities which are calming and leave you feeling refreshed.

Chances are, the day may arrive when no matter what you do, you'll encounter some level of burnout. To put the excitement and fun back into selling, the following are four areas to consider. Evaluate their current place in your way of life and if any of them could use improvement, start an action plan to make the needed changes.

**Give yourself a new beginning.** When we get into a rut, we tend to dwell on it. A new beginning means leaving the past in the past. If you've been the low producer in your organization, stop thinking like the low producer. If you are not calling on enough prospects, stop dwelling on failures and focus on fresh opportunities. Start thinking, acting and talking like the successful sales representative you want to be.

**Change your routine.** Set a complete change into motion. Start with the time you awaken each morning, the time you leave for work, your daytime habits, the order of your work routine, etc. Try taking an early morning walk or trip to the gym. Eat a healthy breakfast. Take a different route on the drive to work. Restructure your workday, avoiding unnecessary interruptions and other time wasters. You can't become what you want to be by keeping the same habits.

**Revamp your schedule.** Connect your daily planner to your goals. Focus on revenue-building activities which translate to face-to-face meetings with new prospects or more telephone time with people who are in your market. Renew your commitment. Chart your progress and never finish a day without giving yourself an honest assessment.

**Take action in your personal life.** Sales slumps can cause, or be the result of, issues outside of work. If you have family at home, make them your first priority. Leave the office at the office. If your finances are the source of stress, take a realistic approach to what needs adjusting in order to cope. There are credit counselors at no cost in your community who can help create a plan for making this area of your life manageable. If needed, take advantage of their help.

17

Being in control of your physical routine and learning how to manage everyday pressure will keep you on the road to success.

## *Your organizational routine*

The silent support for your mental and physical routines is your method of organization. Rounding out your daily system, the items that surround you in your work area and how they pertain to your productivity play a large role in structuring the day to work in your favor.

Many sales representatives struggle with all types of physical clutter—countless piles of paper, numerous unread e-mails, inadequate storage, and no effective process for paper flow and follow-up. The following are areas that frequently need to be evaluated to help keep your organizational routine sound and in check.

### Your desk and briefcase

I have found that assigning a place to store all of my belongings is a smart practice to keep. If you think about it, very few things are misplaced once you have chosen a designated space for them. In terms of your desk drawers, allocate space for business cards, stationery, envelopes, rulers, pens and any other tools necessary to accomplish your daily tasks. Keep like items together and store each type closest to the place where it will be used.

This goes for your desktop as well. Nothing is more frustrating than having to work around several piles of clutter. Allocate space on your desk for the most important file folders and materials pertaining to ongoing proposals, clients and projects. Neatly stack them for easy accessibility and reference. Don't delay filing the remainder. Avoid the mentality, "I'll set this aside for now, it's just temporary." All too often, "temporary" turns into days, days turn into months and soon you'll have a mountain of items to sort through.

Your briefcase is no exception to the rules of neatness and organization. The fact is, perception is reality and people are not only looking at you and your desk, they are also looking at what you carry into meetings. Whether your briefcase is simply a leather portfolio or bears resemblance to a small piece of luggage, keep in mind that it's on display. On a regular basis, clean the briefcase's exterior and replace it when it becomes worn. If papers are spilling out of the pockets, determine how to make them orderly. Recognize that your briefcase is an extension of your desk. The same concept that applies to briefcases pertains to purses. Whether used in tandem with another bag or as the sole method of transporting professional items, a purse should represent its owner in a neat and orderly fashion.

### Your filing system

Studies have shown that up to 85% of documents are never retrieved once filed. It's important to be able to put your fingertips on the other 15%

in a matter of minutes. When it comes to managing your filing system and paper flow, design a process that works for you. It's a well-known fact that more information is delivered on a daily basis than ever before, so it is imperative to set up a system to touch paper once and file each type of document where you know you will be able to find it. A successful rule of mine that you may want to consider is this: *Read the material—delegate or act—file or toss.*

What follows is a simple method to think about when setting up your filing system and paper flow:

- Sort every piece of paper in your work space into files that represent clients or categories.

- Organize the files into order by alphabet, date, number or subject matter. It might be helpful to create an outline of the clients or categories being used and the types of materials contained in each file. This will serve as a future reference as to where various materials are stored.

- Next, appoint a place to store each file. Consider all of the file sizes and how frequently you access them. Obtain the correct size cabinets, shelving or containers.

- And last but not least, don't be afraid to discard papers and materials you know are just taking up space. If necessary, utilize your company's archival storage for anything that you feel might be needed in the future.

**Your calendar**

With the abundance of calendars available today, finding the one that is best for you might take a little effort. While handheld computers, day timers, wall calendars and the latest cell phone technology all hold promise, finding a functional calendar is essential. More importantly, your calendar of choice has to be used and used consistently. Not only will it help keep your schedule on track, a calendar requires you to make choices when it comes to your list of priorities. When you open your calendar, it's readily apparent that there are only twenty-four hours in a day, so each minute of the day had better count.

One of the best tips I have learned when it comes to schedules is that having one master calendar is a good idea. In the past, I would have three or four calendars working at once: one on my desktop, another on my laptop, one on the wall and another in my briefcase—an organizational nightmare. Stick to one master calendar and the odds of overextending yourself and missing important dates will drop greatly.

### Your messaging system

It's a common fact that the clients you visit with over the telephone are just as important as those you meet face-to-face. Knowing this should encourage you to be conscious of the messaging system in place at your corporate office, in your home office or on your cellular telephone. In your absence, your outgoing message is representative of who you are.

Successful salespeople manage their pre-recorded voice messages very well. Is your message current and does it represent you properly? When others call, what do they hear? Flourishing sales professionals record messages that:

- Are spoken slowly and directly into the telephone mouthpiece
- Communicate appreciation and concern for the caller
- Communicate when the caller can expect a return call
- Communicate a friendly, upbeat and informative message

**Example:** *"Hello, this is (your name) with (company name). You have reached my voice mail. Your call is very important to me. Please leave your name, number and a brief message and I will be happy to return your call as soon as possible. If you need immediate assistance, please press zero and speak to the operator. Thank you for your call and I look forward to speaking to you soon. Have a nice day."*

*Helpful Telephone Hints*

❖ When making a call, be prepared to leave a concise message
❖ Answer the telephone with your name
❖ Return all calls or have them returned on your behalf
❖ Smile; it will resonate through your voice
❖ Be friendly before you know who the caller is
❖ Don't be too busy to be courteous; suggest a call-back time if necessary

Once you have recorded your message, play it back and listen to how it sounds. Are you pleased with your representation for all incoming calls? Make it a point to listen to the tone of your voice. Are you upbeat and welcoming? If your message is rushed or not clear, re-record it.

**Your computer system**

Much like anything you organize, how you choose to store electronic files, title documents and folders, back up your system and transfer information from one computer to the next is worth reviewing often. Each person has a different strategy for remaining organized when it comes to a computer. My own filing system is sometimes hit or miss. When I see I have acquired too many icons on my monitor, I know it is time to stop and reorganize.

Things are great when your computer system is working in sync with your other electronic tools, but don't ever take for granted the importance of backing up your work. Not only is it a smart habit to organize documents, presentations, spreadsheets and so forth, it is doubly important to always remember to back up your system to a DVD, external hard drive or server. Set aside a regular time on your calendar each week to organize your technology tools.

**Your automobile**

Okay, so what's the big deal if your home away from home is filthy most of the time? Does it make you any more or any less productive during an average day? I don't know if any studies have ever linked productivity to a clean or dirty vehicle, but doesn't it make you feel better when yours is clean? It goes right back to removing as much clutter as possible.

Whether it is that Happy Meal® sack tucked under the passenger seat, or the accumulation of sand and leaves from climbing in and out, take time to detail your automobile. When your vehicle is in shipshape condition, it gives a feeling of organization and neatness. This alone can improve your attitude from one stop to the next. If it has been raining for eight days straight, you can ignore the exterior—but don't neglect the interior. You never know when the opportunity may arise during a sales call to invite clients to lunch. Imagine the impression you would make if you left them standing outside while you cleared the floorboard and seat. By the same token, your colleagues deserve the same common courtesy. How often do you carpool to a meeting? Take pride in this extension of your office.

Managing your daily responsibilities definitely becomes easier when you can stay on track. Keeping your mental and physical routines orderly and efficient will undeniably bring added structure to each day and increase your productivity. Taking the time to become familiar with the methods that work best for you is a great start to maintaining organization.

## ⟿ CALL TO ACTION ⟾

Spend ten minutes at the end of each day putting everything away. This simple step will allow you to walk into an organized and inviting office each and every morning. Re-evaluate your organizational structure at least biannually or as new assignments are acquired.

Hold an object (pen, ruler, etc.) representing your goal in front of you at eye level and arm's length. Concentrate on the object in the forefront. As you continue focusing, can you distinguish items in the background? Odds are, the answer is yes, but they are blurry and out of focus. You can compare those surroundings to problems and obstacles that will always be present. Now, take your focus off of the central object and focus on the items in the background. As they become clear, the focal point becomes blurred. How can this concept apply to your professional goals?

For the next week, arrive at least five minutes early to all appointments and meetings. Create a chart documenting the reactions you receive from those around you.

23

# 3

# ORGANIZE THE TOOLS YOU DEPEND ON

Just as carpenters depend on their squares, hammers and levels, sales representatives rely on their own unique chests of tools. Even though the types of instruments may differ, the concept is still the same. No one can master a craft without the help of specific tools.

Those who are in the habit of surveying their mental, physical and organizational routines also make it a priority to organize their sales tools quite frequently. Whether in the office or in between bites during a continental breakfast on the road, it behooves you to take inventory of the important items that help make up your sales arsenal.

## *Your tool chest*

In the world of sales, no two tool chests are exactly alike; however, some items continue to be a staple for those who choose to employ them. From the simple to more complex call lists, to all sorts of collateral pieces that educate others on your product or service, effective salespeople stay current while not forgetting to retool when necessary. Let's take a closer look at the various things that make your tool chest more competitive.

**An organized call list**

Establishing the best method of organizing an effective call list should be your first priority when stocking your arsenal. Some refer to this as a prospect list, client list, customer list, business list or just a plain list of people needing to be contacted. Whatever the case may be, for our purposes I'm going to refer to it as a simple call list—a record of existing or potential clients who need to be reached out to.

A call list can be as simple or complex as you choose to make it. No matter what I've ever sold or promoted, I have always believed in structuring this list in the simplest way possible. For example:

| Name | Company | Address | Telephone | Notes |
|------|---------|---------|-----------|-------|
| Janet Carson | Carson Battery | 238 First Street Sacramento, CA | 000-000-0000 | Takes calls on Tuesdays |
| Mark Tilley | Tilley Tires | P.O. Box 35 New York, NY | 000-000-0000 | Office closes at 3:00 |
| Butch Jones | RV Rental | 19990 M Street Detroit, MI | 000-000-0000 | Prefers in-person calls |

When at my desk, on an airplane or between stops in the car, this is one file I pull out often. The inventory of information helps keep me on task and outlines the progress made during a particular day, week or month. The notes jotted down are critical for keeping track of what has already transpired as well as the next call to action. From dollar figures and inventory amounts to names, places and things, it's imperative that much attention be paid to this tool.

No matter how you choose to record this type of information, whether on a computer, personal digital assistant (PDA) or plain piece of paper, keep the data current. You are only as good as the information you have at your fingertips, so keep your list up to speed. Your results depend heavily on how well your tool chest is organized, and your call list is the very foundation from which to begin. If you don't know who to begin reaching out to, odds are you won't be doing much reaching.

### An orderly database

It wasn't but a few short years ago when I realized I had a problem that I couldn't get a handle on. There were numerous opportunities to attend functions where I passed out my business card. Dinners, receptions, trade-shows—you get the picture. The problem was not found in the cards I handed out, but in how I organized the cards received. Here was the opportunity to exchange my information for another's, but at the end of the day I was doing an extremely poor job of keeping up with the information obtained.

For instance, what is the first thing you do with a business card you have received from someone else? After you have scribbled a few brief notes on the back, does the card end up at the bottom of your purse, stuffed down a side pocket in your briefcase, in the inside pocket of your suit jacket, at the top of another plastic sheet housed in a three-ring binder or with the rest of the business cards held together by a rubber band in the top drawer of your desk?

Granted, you might have a system that you have tried to effectively put in place. The important question to answer, though, is: Does the process meet your needs so you can successfully manage your contact base?

Knowing that my original method of dropping cards into the top two drawers of my desk needed to change, I turned to my computer for help. Initially I created a spreadsheet to keep track of the information I received. Much like my call list, the spreadsheet I created included a great deal of important content. This served me well for quite some time, until I located another tool that took my database to the next level.

With the help of a colleague, I was able to design a database that became a solution to my increasing needs—a collection of data that helped me effectively manage the constantly changing information of clients and business contacts. Each field designed within the database had a purpose and was at the tip of my fingers when needing to add or subtract key data. What follows is an example of a basic file outline:

| RECORD 284 | |
| --- | --- |
| **BUSINESS INFORMATION** | |
| FIRST NAME | Gerald |
| LAST NAME | Brumfield |
| TITLE | President |
| COMPANY | Brumfield Implement Company |
| BUSINESS ADDRESS | 488 Marks Drive |
| CITY | Savannah |
| STATE | Georgia |
| ZIP | 31405 |
| COUNTRY | USA |
| BUSINESS PHONE | 000-000-0000 |
| MOBILE PHONE | 000-000-0000 |
| BUSINESS FAX | 000-000-0000 |
| E-MAIL | gbrumfield@bicosavga.com |
| WEBSITE | www.bicosavga.net |
| **PERSONAL INFORMATION** | |
| HOME ADDRESS | 381 Wisteria Circle |
| CITY | Savannah |
| STATE | Georgia |
| ZIP | 31405 |
| HOME PHONE | 000-000-0000 |
| SPOUSE | Sarah |
| BIRTHDAY | November 11 |
| INTERESTS | Golf, deep sea fishing |
| **FOLLOW-UP** | |
| REFERRED BY | Roger Williams |
| CALL BACK | Mid-June |
| NOTES | Initial order—April 2008 Six-month fulfillment |

From spouses' names and birthdays to e-mail addresses and websites, this type of database can serve many different functions within a business. No matter the system and where it is stored, make sure it works for you. If organized properly, this tool will not only help you become more effective, it will assist you in continuing to build your client profiles.

**Valuable collateral pieces**

The collateral pieces that are used to support your product or service are an extension of your sales presentation. From tri-fold brochures to postcards, pamphlets, posters, videos and samples, it is critical that you keep in mind that perception is reality.

When shopping for a product or service, there is nothing as impressive as receiving a packet of information that is crisp and pristine. Regardless of the color combination or design, clients appreciate those who take pride in the appearance of their materials. From hand delivering information to placing it in the mail, whatever arrives on another's desk is an extension of you. As you travel from place to place, make it a point to take care of your collateral.

A good illustration is the trunk of your automobile. If kept neat and clean, your collateral pieces stand a greater chance of staying in mint condition. Some Saturday afternoons I find myself inventorying and restocking all of the materials carried in my trunk. Throwing things away while keeping the bulk of the materials is part of the routine. Don't ever underestimate the importance of keeping your arsenal of tools in excellent condition—ragged edges, fingerprints, torn packaging and those occasional coffee stains all need to be taken into account.

When it comes to your supporting materials, be alert to what works and what doesn't. If you are in a decision-making role regarding the creation of the items that support your cause, keep thinking outside of the box. If you are not part of the creative process, keep your ears open to clients. Listen to what they are expecting to find when opening your brochure or viewing your video. Respectfully pass the knowledge gained to the decision-maker. Looking for ways to better promote your product or service will be appreciated.

29

### Reprinted articles and letters of reference

Whatever product or service you are promoting, the more information you can provide to clients illustrating the worth of their investments, the better. Knowing this, I've always been intrigued by the power of two tools that are at times overlooked—reprinted articles and letters of reference.

You and I understand the value of widespread exposure and sincere accolades. Both can be and are extremely important to the growth of a business. Newspaper articles, magazine editorials and Internet coverage are a few of the resources that help showcase what you stand behind. They highlight your product or service, not only on the day the story is launched, but also during the many months to come. Become as aggressive as possible when searching to find positive articles that pertain to what you represent. Reprint them

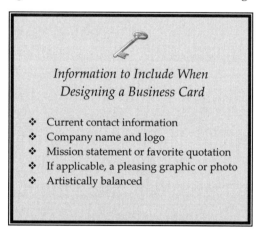

*Information to Include When Designing a Business Card*

❖ Current contact information
❖ Company name and logo
❖ Mission statement or favorite quotation
❖ If applicable, a pleasing graphic or photo
❖ Artistically balanced

and include them with your other collateral. People like to read about the things they are investing in. Not only does it assist them in their educational process, but they see the example others set through their purchase as well.

Sharing praise that existing clientele pass along is no different. If a business professional takes time to write a sincere letter of gratitude for a job well done, convey it to others. Now, when I suggest sharing, I am also suggesting you do it in the proper way—with class and dignity.

Thank you notes or any other correspondence giving affirmation and shining a positive light on you and your product or service matter a great

30

deal. These, too, are excellent tools to place with your other materials. You'd be surprised how many people take time to read the thoughts and opinions of others before ever looking through a brochure or viewing a promotional video.

### Company and personal stationery

One of the best investments you can ever make is purchasing personal stationery. Most companies provide some form of stationery that can be used when following up with existing or prospective clients; others depend on you supplying your own. In either case, don't underestimate the importance of a handwritten note.

I'll share more perspective on this concept in Chapter 10. In the meantime, recognize that a little thanks goes a long way and your company and/or personal stationery are important tools to help convey your debt of gratitude.

31

No matter what is found within your sales arsenal, keep your tool chest organized and current. As an effective sales representative, stay up to date with what is being posted on your organization's website, the mission of the latest television and radio campaign, what images and storylines are being promoted on billboards and in ads, and any current or future product modifications. The more understanding you have—not only of your product or service, but how it is being marketed and promoted—the more successful you will be.

## CALL TO ACTION

Check your business card stash. If you need to reorder, then do so. There is nothing worse than walking into a sales meeting, being offered a business card and not being able to extend the same gesture in return. With as many contacts as you make during an average day, you can never have too many cards on hand.

Before this week ends, update your current call list(s). Include new information and revise existing entries.

Over the next few months, contact your best clients and ask for a letter of referral. When approaching the clients, first ask if they have been pleased with your performance and that of your product or service. Let them know that others in the market are interested in their opinion. If they indicate they were pleased, politely ask them to write a letter at their convenience based on their experience.

# 4

## DEVELOP
## SOUND
## MENTORS

I have come to depend on the advice, opinions and wisdom of others to help me navigate through many major obstacles when dealing with my professional career. These advisors have become sound mentors based on their principles, work ethic and genuine concern for those around them.

Early on, one of the greatest pieces of wisdom I learned was to be conscious of those whom I wanted to model my sales patterns after. I needed to be observant when watching or reading about other more experienced salespeople, and how they established both themselves and their businesses. Watching closely, I learned what habits to form and what habits to avoid.

To gain the wisdom needed to become successful, many sales organizations today ask inexperienced sales representatives to enroll in the "school of hard knocks." Everyone knows trial by fire takes time and has a negative effect on the bottom line as well as the underlying confidence of the salesperson. Companies and organizations that invest time and effort in maintaining and maturing their sales forces believe in the importance of mentoring. Through this approach, many of the common mistakes that hamper sales practices are illustrated and learned from. Sharing the importance of integrity, rapport, composure and intuition, mentors give junior sales reps an edge when coming out of the starting gate.

## The value of integrity

The quality of possessing and adhering to high moral principles and professional standards is one of the most complete definitions I have found for integrity. Existing or potential clients would much rather deal with a sales representative who is honest and straightforward, versus one who is not. In an age where corporate greed, fraudulent transactions and all sorts of scandals headline the news, the value of integrity is more appreciated now than ever. When looking for individuals to model your sales patterns after, search for ones who have integrity—not only when representing their products or services, but more importantly when representing themselves.

If you say you are going to do something, then do it. If you can't, then don't make empty promises. If you inform clients of specifics surrounding a delivery and for whatever reason schedules change, immediately contact them. If you place callers on hold and say, "I'll be right back," then make sure you return quickly and don't leave them wondering if they've been forgotten.

These and hundreds of other examples and scenarios can all be linked to the word integrity. Your word represents your name. Your name represents your product or service. Your success rate hinges on many values—one being integrity.

## The value of rapport

Successful salespeople are continually working on building sincere relationships that can withstand the everyday changes and uncertainties of business trends and environments. No matter what you sell or promote, always remember you make your living by connecting with others. Knowing this is incentive to look for those mentors who have the ability to build strong relationships that endure.

I found a good example of this value during the time I spent working for a marketing firm early in my career. The firm prided itself on a versatile list of clientele. Yet, over the years it was extremely successful in carving out one particular market niche that it became well known for. There were many reasons this transpired, but one of the biggest was the ability to build rapport with clients. The relationships built didn't last for a year or two; they lasted for what seemed a lifetime. The firm was and is able to maintain this level of success because its clients are more than customers, they are friends—and with friendship comes a great deal of loyalty. It was rewarding to be a part of an organization that not only concentrated on the bottom line, but also on building strong bonds that increased the value of what we were selling and the relationships we were establishing.

35

## _The value of composure_

Anyone who has ever walked into a prospective client's place of business and, after a brief introduction, was shown the door understands the real value of composure. It isn't necessary to encounter this often for you to recall the embarrassment, frustration and true feeling of rejection that emerge when being reminded of such an experience.

I remember the first time an incident like this occurred in my sales career. I was working on a magazine project selling advertising space when I walked into an establishment and asked for the owner.

I vividly recall the owner approaching the counter as I led into a brief introduction of myself and the magazine I was representing. I did not have three sentences out of my mouth before the gentleman asked, "Are you a salesman?"

I will never forget that question. I replied, "Yes sir, I am."

As I began to continue, he quickly stopped me again and said, "I don't like where you parked your car."

Somewhat puzzled, I asked, "I'm sorry?"

With a hint of irritation in his voice, he repeated, "I don't like where you parked your car!"

"Sir," I said, "I'm the only car in your parking lot."

The owner then said, "You're right." And with that he asked me to get into my car and leave.

I can't tell you how embarrassed and frustrated I was by being rejected. To this day, I can still remember how it felt to have the eyes of the owner and his staff staring right at me as I exited the door. I can only imagine how my blood pressure would have measured at that moment.

It is times like these when it is imperative to react with composure. One of my closest business advisors has always reminded me that through a calm, steady and composed response, I have the ability to react to what has to be done, when it needs to be done, for as long as it takes. Circumstances will continuously occur and individuals will act and react in various ways. You might not be able to control how others react, but you certainly can control your reaction.

My first experience with being dismissed was also my first opportunity to react with composure. Yes, I was irritated that day, frustrated and perhaps even angry that I was treated so poorly and not given a chance. But I never lost my poise. As I was leaving, I turned around and looked the owner directly in the eye and said, "Sir, thank you for your time…and have a nice day."

With this incident, I had learned a new level of composure. It taught me the importance of biting my tongue and remaining calm under the most difficult of situations. In the end, I gained more from this sales call than if I had made the sale.

## The value of intuition

"Always trust your instincts when dealing with the behavior of others." This is some of the greatest advice I ever received from those who had my best interest in mind.

As we have come to learn, selling or promoting anything is about building relationships

> ### Words from the Wise
>
> ❖ Follow-through is crucial; don't wait for your customer to call—you call first
> ❖ Be punctual 100% of the time; it will demonstrate your respect for others
> ❖ Always make it a habit to listen more than you speak
> ❖ You will never know the answer unless you ask the question
> ❖ Be consistent in your actions and with your words
> ❖ Keep a journal of all the sales lessons you learn
> ❖ Surround yourself with knowledgeable people
> ❖ Recognize when it is time to change your strategy
> ❖ Do the right thing first and you will never have to second guess yourself

37

and mastering the arts of communication and persuasion. Always keep in mind how the person sitting across the table from you feels. When you think of that person first, you are on the right track to building a quality relationship. Listen to your instincts. Be aware of your surroundings and how they affect all verbal and non-verbal communication. Though you might find value in touting your product or service to an extreme, always be conscious of the temperament of the person to whom you're giving your pitch—before, during and after your presentation.

The ability to recognize another's body language can help validate the information being received. Successful sales representatives recognize that there are many types of body language:

- **Handshakes** — It's possible to learn a lot from someone's handshake. From how long individuals hold the handshake, to the temperature of their skin, to those who do or do not make eye contact during the process, a handshake can give initial insight to a client's receptiveness.

- **Breathing** — Some people breathe quickly and others slowly. Some have a repetitive rhythm to their breathing: deep breath, pause, deep breath. Others' breaths are quick and shallow. How someone breathes is really not that important. What is important is trying to spot a change in a breathing pattern. A deviation is the signal that a person's internal communication state has changed and the level of rapport has fluctuated.

- **Facial expressions** — A face represents the emotions being experienced. Smiles, tears, knitted eyebrows, tense jaws: Reading these types of highly visible facial expressions is familiar territory. However, in the business world, people rarely express their true emotions outwardly. You have only small variations of customers' facial expressions to study. Pay very close attention.

- **Facial color** — Skin color can also give subtle clues to a person's emotional and physical state. In a tense meeting, you may witness the skin tone of someone turn bright red. If the room is stuffy or uncomfortable, you may notice an individual becoming pale. Just as emotion will influence how you are received, physical discomfort can make the difference in closing a sale.

- **Body posture** — A person's body posture is one of the primary features of the physical communication layer. Regardless of the activity (sitting, standing or walking), a person's body posture sends a message to everyone. People are normally in a continual pose and the manner in which they hold and shape their figure reflects their mental state.

Integrity, rapport, composure and intuition are four traits learned from mentors that are consistently found in effective salespeople. It's important to realize, though, much more can be learned from them. The value of maintaining solid relationships with advisors throughout your career cannot be overstated.

I am grateful to the mentors I have absorbed wisdom from over the years. Not only have they taught me what not to do, they've advised me on ways to maximize my potential.

Successful people usually want to help you succeed. Learning what has worked for others can illuminate the pathway of opportunity. Don't be afraid to talk to your mentors and ask what measures they took to achieve success. For mentors, there is no better compliment than knowing that they are admired and their wisdom is desired. Trusted advisors will do everything in their power to increase your likelihood for success.

## CALL TO ACTION

If you have not found a mentor, maybe now is the time. Look for someone to gather wisdom from and increase your progress in sales.

Re-evaluate your handshake. What kind of message do you send when you shake another person's hand? Do you look the individual in the eye? Do you extend your hand first? Is your grip firm and friendly?

If you do not have a sales journal, start one today. Go to the bookstore and purchase a simple journal or tablet. Reflect over the past six months, listing your successes as well as your failures. Find one or two lessons you can take from each experience and begin compiling your own tips for success.

# 5

# UNDERSTAND WHAT YOUR NAME IS ATTACHED TO

How many times have you asked yourself, "What do I, as a sales representative, need to know about my product or service?" Your immediate and recurring answer should be, "Everything!"

Complete product knowledge is essential to a full understanding of what you are attaching your name to. It's a hard and fast fact that at times, some salespeople do not know as much as they should about their products or services. Whatever your own level of knowledge, you should continuously strive to gain as many facts, statistics and benefits as possible about what you are offering to the world.

Why is this so incredibly important? Sales representatives who fully understand what they are promoting build credibility and confidence in the mind of the customer. The salesperson that does not have answers to basic questions raises doubt and, in turn, there is a negative effect on the bottom line.

Not only does product knowledge build customer confidence, it also helps to build self-confidence. As I alluded to earlier, having confidence in yourself as you enter different sales situations is a must. When you, as a sales representative, do not completely grasp your product or service, the client picks up on it quickly. You have enough to think about during a sales presentation without the added concern of not being able to answer the customer's next question.

## *Nothing but the facts*

To assist you with ready access to the knowledge you need, creating a fact sheet outlining the specifics of the product or service being represented is an excellent idea.

A fact sheet, much like a call list, can be as simple or complex as you choose to make it. Let's consider what to include. The following are examples of specific questions that would need to be included if you were a salesperson at a hotel property:

### *Room-related*
What are check-in and checkout times?
What is the property's total number of rooms?
What is the breakdown of smoking and non-smoking rooms?
What is the property's total number of suites?
What amenities are offered?

### *Location-related*
What is the property's total number of parking spaces?
Is there motor coach parking?
What is the distance from the airport?
Is there a complimentary airport shuttle?
What major attractions are located in the same vicinity as the property?

*Restaurant-related*

Does the property have a lounge?

What is the type of food served?

What are the hours of operation?

Is room service offered?

What is the price range by meal?

Is there a continental breakfast?

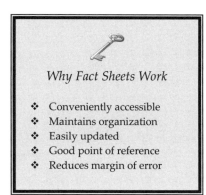

*Why Fact Sheets Work*

❖ Conveniently accessible
❖ Maintains organization
❖ Easily updated
❖ Good point of reference
❖ Reduces margin of error

*Meeting space-related*

Does the property have meeting space available?

How many people can the space accommodate?

What is the total number of meeting rooms?

What are the dimensions and ceiling heights of each room?

Is there built-in equipment (i.e., screens, projectors, etc.)?

Are the meeting rooms Internet accessible?

43

This is just one example of the type of information that might be found on a fact sheet. Your sheet should be created based on specific data pertaining to your product or service as well as answers to previous questions from customers. In addition, there are a few inquiries that apply to every product or service that should always be answered. They include:

- What are the benefits of purchasing my product or service?
- Who would be most interested in what I am promoting?
- How can my product or service help the bottom line of the buyer?
- What have others said about their experience interacting with me?
- What is my company's track record?

The more pertinent information you can include on your list, the better. Different sales representatives jot down various facts; what is important is that they are jotting something down. Put yourself in the customer's shoes when gathering data on what you have to offer. There is no doubt that a salesperson armed with good knowledge and understanding is in a much better position professionally than an individual who is not.

## Be present on the cutting edge

Complete product knowledge is an ongoing process. While many opportunities may be present for learning as much as you can about your specific offering, your education shouldn't end with in-house training or spec sheets from the manufacturer. You've heard the phrase "cutting edge" applied to many different circumstances. Have you ever considered what it takes to be on the cutting edge?

First, being in tune with your product or service means keeping a close eye on the surrounding industry. There are several ways this can be accomplished. Conduct frequent Internet searches for indicators showing trends and modifications within your industry. When you notice a change, begin delving into the reasons this is occurring. Learn as much as you can and apply that knowledge to the situation.

Subscribe to trade journals, newsletters, ezines and insider reports. Take advantage of training updates, market and trade shows, and factory open houses. You'll encounter a lot of knowledge that you may not need to apply immediately, but seeing the larger picture will keep you fresh and edgy. Look for opportunities to attend continuing education courses, whether presented through your company, a manufacturer or a related association. It is likely that many are offered in your field.

Broaden your knowledge base and network by considering membership in an association related to your industry—whether local, regional or national. Stepping outside your comfort zone and reaching out to others in your field will give you an added edge when it comes to promoting your product or service. You may feel your life is chaotic enough; you don't have time to bother with association membership—and then there are the dues. In reality, time spent increasing your knowledge and bettering your skills is time well spent. Any associated cost is small in comparison to the benefits you'll receive. Diverse memberships, shared experiences, industry networking and gained friendships are added dividends to aligning yourself with an association.

You'll meet individuals who share a common interest and from that, strength and added self-confidence will be derived. Priceless information touching on the topics that affect your industry; breaking news on legislation, upcoming meetings, seminars and conventions; and the latest and most proven methods of advertising are just a few ways association membership places you on the cutting edge. Membership usually includes a listing in the association directory. This alone can be beneficial to you in more ways than one.

45

Not only does the directory promote the services of members within the association, in many cases it is distributed outside of the network, increasing opportunities for business. The association has the ability to promote you and your product or service to the right people through various outlets. Keep in mind that most associations have liaisons in the media as well as government agencies.

Finally, many associations have frequent meetings to discuss topics of concern and brainstorm ways to advance and improve. Conventions, award ceremonies, competitions and workshops all share an enormous amount of information, promotion and networking that can be gained through association membership.

Being present on the cutting edge entails sharing knowledge and new ideas while allowing room for improvement. Taking an active role in educating others—whether your client, colleague or someone who is just entering the field—keeps you sharp and outstanding in your industry.

## Be an unmistakable ambassador

Each day that you are provided the opportunity to walk this earth is another day you are given the privilege to be an unmistakable ambassador for what it is you are selling and promoting.

I'm sure you have heard the philosophy: "You are the initial product. Since this is the case, you need to sell yourself as well as your product or service."

I believe wholeheartedly in this theory! Think about it for a moment. Your name is connected to anything you say or do. Whether in the office or on the road, every telephone call, text message, e-mail or face-to-face encounter has your name attached.

46

A few short years ago, I attended a sales training that highlighted this philosophy. During the class, one of the presenters simply stated: "People don't care how much you know—until they know how much you care. Individuals buy from those who make them feel at ease. The very first thing you need to sell to a prospective client is yourself. It is usually the aspect the customer knows the least about, but ultimately will buy."

Allow existing and potential clients to see the real you. For instance, when you are smiling and excited about what you are representing, clients see this and soak it in. They are left with the vibe that you enjoy what you do and through that, your product or service will shine. I can recall an excellent example of this during a recent tour of NBC Studios.

There were two interns, a young man and woman, responsible for providing our group with in-depth knowledge about the specifics surrounding a typical day at NBC. Starting with where the news is reported, to various control rooms and the studio of "Saturday Night Live," both shared facts and trivia we all enjoyed.

Their smiles were contagious as they moved aside to let us step into the elevator or while they escorted the group down one hallway and through the next. As they took turns presenting short narratives at each stop, not only were they shining a light on the network, they were shining light on themselves. Observing their pure enthusiasm for what they represented, our interest was piqued and we were eager to learn more. It was evident that these two young professionals not only enjoyed what they did, but also cared about those on the tour. They fully understood what their name was attached to and took pride in being unmistakable ambassadors.

It doesn't matter if you are completing an internship, if you are a new employee or a seasoned veteran; the product or service you tout deserves nothing but your best. You are the initial product.

47

Understanding what your name is attached to pays ongoing dividends to both you and your customers. The more facts, statistics and benefits offered, the more knowledge your customer has to make a logical decision. To that end, expanding your range of expertise through ramping up your industry involvement is a bonus as well.

As long as you continue to welcome the opportunity to learn and expand within your chosen field, the panoramic view of your sales career will be increasingly brighter. This is essential because the attitude, enthusiasm and eagerness you project will always highlight the product or service you represent.

## ∼◦CALL TO ACTION◦∼

General or extensive, formulate a fact sheet. If one already exists, review it to make sure the information is accurate and to the point.

Create a list of associations that you should consider membership in. Research each organization thoroughly for the benefits or disadvantages before investing your dollars.

Before traveling to your next face-to-face sales call, take a moment to look into a mirror. Ask yourself this one important question: "Am I a good example of an unmistakable ambassador for my product or service?" Once you have the answer…go make the sale.

# 6

## PUT YOUR RIVALS TO WORK FOR YOU

Why do athletic teams send coaches to scout opponents a week before the big game? Why do some companies study the business philosophies of others? Why is one military so concerned with the strategy of another?

The answers to such questions can be summed up with one definite idea: We all want to learn as much as we can about our competition.

The term competition—a major focus for the successful salesperson—is defined as the activity of doing something with the goal of outperforming others.

Today more than ever, the global economy offers a variety of options. No matter what industry you represent, competitors are around most corners. In order to encourage prospective clients to purchase your product or service, it is vital to realize what choices the customer has. When concentrating on the competition, one of your goals should be to discover what your rivals do well and then expand your own strengths to provide the customer a choice. When clients see a distinct difference between your strengths and that of your competitors, they can then make an educated decision, not one solely based on price.

It is extremely important to understand early on who or what you are competing against. Discovering this answer and refining it as the business climate changes will help you to learn as much about the competition as you've learned about yourself. Grasping knowledge of your rivals' strengths and weaknesses from the customer's point of view gives you a distinct advantage when pitching your product or service:

- What are the unique strengths of my product or service?
- What is the added value I offer?
- Can I deliver my product or service in a timely and effective manner?

These are questions that need to be answered by you quickly and concisely. Through your educated reply, the distinguishable differences between your product or service and that of the competition can be accurately communicated to the customer. As an ambassador for what you represent, it is your responsibility to convey information about the unique strengths that make up your point of difference.

## First look inward

Many types of strengths can be identified in your quest to outperform your rivals. It is up to you to recognize their significance and utilize them to elevate your product or service over that of your competitors. Consider the following ten areas of potential strength:

**Overall product:**    The unique characteristics that are evident when setting your product or service apart from others.

| | |
|---|---|
| **People:** | The individuals on your team who go above and beyond in the eyes of the customer. |
| **Customer care:** | The timeliness and consistency of quality customer service offered. |
| **Value versus price:** | The value of the product or service in comparison to price. |
| **Proven experience:** | The length of time you and your business have promoted and sold a certain product or service. |
| **Reputation:** | How your product or service is perceived in the marketplace. |
| **Location:** | The benefit of your location over that of the competition. |
| **Collateral pieces:** | How your marketing tools measure up against your rivals'. |
| **Ironclad guarantee:** | The effectiveness of the guarantee offered to the customer. |
| **You:** | The selling skills you possess and your unique qualifications. |

51

Isolate each of these facets and put them to work for you. How can this be achieved? Create a simple grading method and take a long look at both your rivals' practices and your own.

The following is an example of a basic report card that can be created to help you make an honest comparison between you and your major competitors. Comparing your rivals' strengths to your own as well as determining the reasons for the differences will enable you to improve immensely. In addition, successful sales representatives make it a priority to rate not only themselves, but the company they represent. It is recommended you separately evaluate each one of your major competitors.

| FACET | GRADE | REASON |
|-------|-------|--------|
| Overall product | ☐ We're Stronger  ☐ They're Stronger | |
| People | ☐ We're Stronger  ☐ They're Stronger | |
| Customer care | ☐ We're Stronger  ☐ They're Stronger | |
| Value versus price | ☐ We're Stronger  ☐ They're Stronger | |
| Proven experience | ☐ We're Stronger  ☐ They're Stronger | |
| Reputation | ☐ We're Stronger  ☐ They're Stronger | |
| Location | ☐ We're Stronger  ☐ They're Stronger | |
| Collateral pieces | ☐ We're Stronger  ☐ They're Stronger | |
| Ironclad guarantee | ☐ We're Stronger  ☐ They're Stronger | |
| You | ☐ We're Stronger  ☐ They're Stronger | |

52

Naturally, there are a number of other attributes that can be added to your report card. In any case, you see the pattern forming.

In addition to an evaluation such as this, it is imperative to continually answer other questions that help set you apart from your competition, such as:

- I am the only one who will…
- I am truly unique because…
- The reasons my customers will buy from me are…

This type of exercise will lend a hand when seeking ways to expand your strengths. When making comparisons between yourself and your competition, capitalizing on the information learned will put your rivals to work for you.

## *Scout your rivals*

Just as coaches do before the big game, scouting your opponents is key to putting together your master game plan. Understanding that circumstances vary, it may be difficult for only one person to monitor who or what you are competing against. When possible, don't hesitate to make this a shared responsibility among all your colleagues. Smart salespeople either make it a priority for themselves or delegate others to observe competitors on a continual basis.

Here are some simple ways to take an objective look at your rivals:

**Watch:**  View their Web and media (television, radio and newspaper) presence regularly.

**Read:**  Research trade publications, magazines and other news sources for stories on the companies or industries you are scouting. Sign up for their monthly newsletters.

**Listen:**  Pay attention to what others are saying about your opponents.

53

Staying on top of your competition translates into outperforming its product or service. When you do this consistently, you will definitely see positive results.

## *Now look outward*

Aware of your competitors' positions, armed with your strengths and conscious of your weaknesses, structure a plan for surpassing your rivals. To begin, list the areas previously identified that need improvement. Next, define the steps you will take to correct and advance your position. How does your opponent execute better than you?

As you find yourself reinforcing your weak areas, take another look at your exceptional strengths. How can you leverage those strengths to your advantage? What approach will you take when competing against an opponent who is equal to you in every discernible area? What is your point of difference?

Questions such as these are crucial as you look outward to develop your sales plan. Only you will be able to determine the best solutions. Keep in mind, your rivals are most likely observing you as closely as you are watching them.

Consider the following scenario. Mr. Clark, a patron of many years, has suddenly decided to give his business to the competition across town. Knowing that you consistently score higher than this particular opponent in all areas, at first glance, you assume the client made his decision after receiving a lower price. During a lunch meeting with a colleague, you receive information that leads you to believe that your competitor "stole" your customer through less than ethical practices. Not only have you lost a client, your reputation has been called into question. How will you respond? What can you do to clear up the misunderstanding without sinking to the level of your rival? How can you regain your customer's trust as well as his business?

The example above is just one of countless situations you may encounter throughout your sales career. There will be many different conditions that will necessitate having a well-defined strategy in place in order to stay one step ahead of your competition. When developing yours, it is best to consider and include every possible situation well before it occurs. In doing this, you can see the proper measures that should be taken without your vision being clouded by emotion. This holds true for positive as well as negative encounters with clients, competitors and associates.

A simple analogy can be found on the football field. Each time a team gains possession of the ball, it has four possible attempts at maintaining that possession, whether to advance the ball or score. Though the head coach is ready with the next call from the playbook based on the probable outcome of the current situation, he always has a backup playlist if things don't unfold the way he had planned. Nothing is left to chance.

Your sales strategy is your playbook. Develop it thoroughly, look outward frequently, reference it often, and refine it based on experience and necessity. A well thought-out playbook will serve you effectively during both calm and difficult times. As you construct your methods,

*Traits of Ineffective Sales Representatives*

❖ Overlooking the competition
❖ Not possessing the right mental attitude
❖ Failing to follow up
❖ Becoming preoccupied by distractions
❖ Allowing sales tools to become disorganized
❖ Choosing not to listen first
❖ Not delivering on past promises
❖ Lacking a true belief in the product or service
❖ Failing to stay in contact with past customers

remember—what is most important is not just making one sale, but creating relationships that will encourage clients to return again and again. Your strategy will determine your success.

55

Having knowledge of yourself and your rivals, along with a well-structured sales strategy, is of no benefit if not set into motion. Proper implementation and execution will give you an added advantage over your competition.

There is no doubt you will gain important knowledge about your competitors' practices through an inward evaluation process and balanced scouting. Now is the time to apply what you've learned in your outward approach. Discover the techniques that complement your sales strategy and always be willing to refine the information acquired. Every day you step onto the playing field is one more day you have to listen, learn and lean on the unique facets that make you and your business one of a kind.

## ∽ CALL TO ACTION ∼

Using the example report card found on page 52, separately evaluate five of your major rivals. Aware of each competitor's position, list the primary areas where you and your business need improvement. Next, define the steps you will take to correct and advance your position.

During the next week, pick an evening and search the Internet for any videos that provide pertinent information on the strengths or weaknesses of your opponents.

Create your sales playbook. Beginning with report cards, lists of answers to important questions and all other information that is vital to the success of your sales strategy, start compiling a well-organized playbook. Index all materials and consider adding other components from your tool chest.

# 7

## BE AWARE
## OF YOUR
## APPEARANCE

Many variables will influence the number of existing and prospective clients you have at any one time. Standing head and shoulders above your competition involves much more than good tools and a wealth of information. Undoubtedly attitude, work ethic, knowledge and honesty all play a major role in being a top producer. No matter how strong your total package is, the first impression you make will influence customers' opinions throughout all dealings, perhaps even dictating whether they will purchase at all.

No doubt you have heard throughout your life, "Don't judge a book by its cover." I totally agree with this philosophy. However, the sore reality is that a customer's first impression is strongly dictated by your outer appearance. People draw conclusions very quickly. What message do you want your appearance to project?

We all know people who, no matter where they are or what they are doing, simply look great. They seem to have a certain sense of style that some call "the look." You might say they have a knack for dressing. This sounds so mysterious, but in reality it's very simple.

What is their secret? They are consistently neat, appropriate and well-groomed. By following these simple rules, not only will you make a good first impression, you too will be in a position to always look your best.

When defining your own positive image, begin by asking yourself this question: What is my best appearance asset, and how can I build on it? Whatever it is, use it properly and develop it to your best advantage. If in doubt, ask the opinion of your family and closest friends. If you need the assistance of a professional stylist to determine what is most effective for you, consider it an investment that will pay off on a daily basis. Let's take a look at the factors that contribute to presenting yourself in the best possible light.

58

**Neatness** — Neatness counts. Being neat is an often overlooked part of creating the total look. When I speak of neatness, I'm not talking only about the clothing you wear, but about you—your total package. You are selling not only your abilities and product or service, you are also presenting yourself.

**Hairstyle** — Your hairstyle will immediately be one of the first items of your appearance that will be evaluated. Is it neat? Is it fresh? Is it natural? Do you have to constantly brush hair out of your eyes? Does your hair have

*Invest in You*

❖ Evaluate your wardrobe
❖ Update your eyewear
❖ Consider changing hairstyles
❖ Polish your shoes

a style, and is it appropriate for the type of business you represent? Some individuals like to assert their individuality through their hairstyle. You will find a greater level of success if you let your personality, intelligence and innermost self tell others about the unique individual that you are.

**Attire** — Your attire speaks volumes about you. If your clothing is wrinkled or your general appearance is disheveled, this screams that you are not an orderly person and you do not pay attention to details. Dressing appropriately is of the essence. Just because something is in style does not make it appropriate when representing yourself and your product or service. This is especially important when putting together your overall look. Bear in mind, this is not the time to make a political statement, advertise personal viewpoints or highlight your social differences. In all situations, modesty is the best bet. It isn't necessary to spend an exorbitant amount of money on your wardrobe. Whether your budget is large or small, if you select your clothing with good taste and an eye for professionalism, you will achieve a look of style and success. Whether you shop at the local thrift store or a high-end boutique, there are plenty of brands and choices that will fit the need.

**Shoes** — When wrapping up the details, don't forget your shoes. Be sure that they are clean and shined and show a "well-cared-for" appearance. Take care that the heels are not worn down, and that the seams are intact. They should be coordinated to your outfit, and not extreme in any way. Your attention to detail in all things is what will make the difference between success and failure.

59

**Accessories** — It is said that accessories can make or break an outfit. They can also make—or break—a first impression. While jewelry can be a nice addition to your total look, inappropriate or excessive use can be a distracting factor and influence your client's opinion in a positive or negative way. Exercise moderation when selecting the accessories you wear each day. As an added note, first impressions are impacted by facial piercings more than any other self-imposed physical feature. If facial piercings are something you enjoy having, seek ways to minimize their appearance when meeting with your clientele. Practice moderation when you are putting your professional foot forward.

**Cleanliness** — Almost certainly, the most important part of dressing well is being clean and odor-free. This includes both you and your clothing. Be selective when choosing your attire for the day. Look for stains, small tears, broken stitches and holes. If you think it won't be noticed, it probably will. You saw it, didn't you? Give your clothing the sniff test. If it looks clean but has an odor, it is not clean. Does it smell like tobacco smoke from the restaurant you visited the other evening? Does it have that fishy smell that comes from being outside in the heat and humidity? If it isn't immaculate in look and smell, don't wear it until it is as fresh to the nose as it is to the eye.

**Dental hygiene** — It is important to not only be fresh, clean and odor-free in body and attire, but also to be fully aware of your dental hygiene. Take special care that you do not have foul breath. Keep a toothbrush and toothpaste in your desk, car or briefcase to freshen up after a coffee, smoke or lunch break. Always have breath mints on hand. There are few things worse than having to back away during a conversation due to another person's halitosis. Not only is it a distraction to the client, but the natural reaction will be to turn away.

60

**Finishing touch** — Don't forget the seemingly smallest of details: Fingernails that are clean, well-groomed and absent of extreme polish will make your hands more presentable. Avoid heavy makeup and highly scented cologne or aftershave. Be conscious of facial hair, not to exclude your nose, eyebrows and ears. Your clients will not only appreciate your appearance, but be able to focus on the product or service you are presenting without distractions.

Despite how well-groomed or nicely dressed you are, there is one action that can undo all of your hard work when defining your personal image—the act of encroaching on another's personal space. For instance, have you ever been around individuals who crowded your space? These people may have been pleasant, but when they got close to you there was some mannerism or aspect of their persona that made you want to turn around and walk quickly in the other direction. Or perhaps, they just got too close.

Case in point: Andrew was a member of a sales team for a company that manufactured baby products. Once a week, the entire sales team met to brainstorm ways to expand sales of the various products produced. A manager who had been with the company for approximately five years, Andrew was very sociable and quick to share good ideas with the group. At the beginning of each gathering, he would typically greet each person in the room with a firm handshake or a slap on the back. He was well-groomed and nicely dressed and his overall appearance was appropriate for his position with the company.

However, Andrew had a very annoying habit during one-on-one conversations of getting right in the faces of people he was speaking to, encroaching on their personal space without respect for their desire to have some "breathing room." A heavy coffee drinker, Andrew seemed unaware his breath reeked of the three cups he consumed on the way to the office. Oblivious to the effect he was having on his colleagues, Andrew would press forward until his co-workers made excuses and walked away.

61

When seated at the conference table, Andrew made a habit of pulling his nail clippers from his suit pocket and using the opportunity during the meeting to clean underneath his fingernails. As if not bad enough, without fail at least once during the meeting he would sneeze, remove his handkerchief from his trousers and blow his nose. Understandably, it is difficult to control when and where a sneeze takes place; however, what can be controlled is the manner in which one tends to it. In Andrew's case, the handkerchief always looked like it was three days past time to be laundered, never mind that he made it a point to shake your hand (without first washing his) one last time before the meeting adjourned. No matter how jovial he was, most of his colleagues avoided him like the plague due to his habits.

## TAKE YOUR APPEARANCE PULSE

You have one opportunity to make a positive initial impact on your client. What image are you trying to project? Honestly reflect on each of the following questions.

| | |
|---|---|
| How do I dress? | |
| Where do I need to improve? | |
| How often do I brush my teeth after lunch? | |
| Do I launder my handkerchief daily? | |
| Am I what my customer perceives? | |
| How can I make a better first impression? | |
| How does my appearance impact the business? | |
| Does my appearance say anything about my attitude toward my job? | |
| What subtle changes can I make to improve my overall appearance? | |
| How often do I encroach on another's personal space? | |

Although your appearance may make up the majority of your persona, your approachability creates a level of comfort for your customer. Pride and attention to detail translate to pride in your profession and the product or service you represent. Take into account the factors shared within this chapter as they relate to your patron's first and lasting impression of you. Never underestimate the influence your appearance has at any given time or during any given situation.

## ～◈ CALL TO ACTION ◈～

If you have not completed your appearance pulse on page 62, now is a good time to do so. By taking a moment to make an honest self-assessment and act on any changes you deem necessary, you will not only increase your sales potential, you will increase your self-esteem.

Re-examine how you approach the personal space of others. Do you put enough distance between the person you are speaking to and yourself?

63

Lend a hand to another. If close friends or co-workers are constantly invading the space of others or have an issue with cleanliness or dental hygiene, share your concern with them. As long as you approach this in a respectful and non-threatening manner, your colleagues might flinch at first, but will be grateful at the end of the day.

# 8

## Seek Out New Business Leads

History has shown that one of the main reasons sales representatives consistently fail is because they do not spend enough time standing on the front steps of their business seeking out new customers. For many sales professionals, the toughest step is the first one right out of their own front door.

To have a fair chance at being successful in promoting or selling anything, you must not only take this all-important first step, but be willing to go far beyond. This smart practice was extremely apparent when I had the chance to travel to Rome, Italy for the first time.

"Buongiorno," shop owners would say as they stood at the entrances to an assortment of boutiques, coffee bars and cafés. "How may I help you?" or "What would you like?" they asked with big grins and energetic smiles. A true feeling of hospitality could be felt as I began to experience individuals proud to extend to me opportunities to learn more about their products or services. It wasn't as if I or anyone else had to stand in one place for a long period of time waiting to be noticed or attended to.

Shop owners, maître d's and salespeople representing their products or services were actively seeking new customers—not intrusively, but with "eager to serve you" attitudes.

Those successful in sales make it a priority to leave their office and seek out business at least two days a week, if not more. Now let's be realistic, it is quite difficult at times to leave your desk for an hour-long meeting down the hallway, let alone a day or two a week. I can't tell you how many times I've been told, "It's next to impossible to get away. There are just too many things that need to be done."

Though there will always be exceptions, that argument no longer holds much water. With the latest advances in technology, there are more ways than ever before to stay connected to the office. Whether in Rome or anywhere else, no matter how much you need to do, you can't afford not to leave the office and actively seek out new leads.

When stepping outside of your office, you have the opportunity to network and meet with prospective clients in their environments. Through these encounters, you learn what is most important to them, why your product or service meets their needs, and any areas that may still need improvement. You have to do your best to locate qualified leads. This takes great diligence and resolve. Many salespeople find difficulty in hitting their overall goals because they do not know where to find quality prospects. They also struggle with differentiating between leads with great potential and those that are a drain on time.

That brings me to this one precise question: "Where do you begin to locate quality prospects for your product or service?" There is no doubt this one question holds many valuable responses—all worth the effort to examine closely. The first time I was asked this question, I noted three primary answers: previous clients, existing clients and accessible resources. Let's explore this further.

## *Previous clients*

When challenged with the task of digging up new leads, there is no better place to begin than with customers who did business with you and your organization in the past. Depend on your database, previous contracts, old call lists, notes, letters or whatever information can be resurrected. Just because clients stopped giving you their business doesn't mean they might not consider providing you with another opportunity.

Approach it in this manner. There are a multitude of reasons customers discontinue doing business with you—buying habits change, competitors come and go, mergers take place. Whatever the case, if you have done business with clients in the past and you met or exceeded their expectations, odds are they will give you another chance.

Don't be afraid to reach out and renew past relationships. Pick up the telephone, write a letter, knock on the door; put forth the effort to let these important people know you care. As you develop leads from your previous client base, keep in mind there will be situations needing to be addressed:

67

- If their business was lost due to a misstep on your end, let them know it has been addressed and improvements have been made.
- If they stopped doing business with you without explanation, politely ask why and then follow that question with, "What can I do to earn your business again?"
- If the investment in your product or service did not fit within the parameters of their budget, share with them any upcoming sales or discounted offers.

These types of communications will not only provide you keen insight into the mind of the customer, it might very well give you the chance to add a new name to your current client list while striking one from your old.

## Existing clients

The next group to turn your attention toward is existing clients. Who better to call on for assistance when seeking out new leads, testimonials or recommendations? No one knows your product or service better than current, satisfied customers who invest their hard-earned money in what you offer. This expenditure gives them a vested interest in your success and their pride of ownership will usually extend to helping in the expansion of your business.

I was once given a simple piece of advice from a sales representative who was in the habit of continually increasing his customer base. On the way back to the office from an afternoon meeting, he and I were in deep conversation about how to identify new business leads. Chuck offered this idea: "How many times during one day do you sit down for a meal?"

I answered, "Normally, twice. Once at lunch and once at dinner."

68

*Positive Listening Skills*

❖ Give undivided attention
❖ Evaluate content of message—not the messenger
❖ Be silent until a person finishes speaking
❖ Don't complete another person's sentence
❖ Adopt an active body language
❖ Control or eliminate distractions
❖ Keep an open mind—ask questions to clarify

Then Chuck asked, "Who do you normally share your meals with, fellow colleagues, friends, your family?"

"To be quite honest," I replied, "it just depends on what's going on that day."

"Well then, if that's the case," he said, "I want you to ask yourself something. How often do you pick up the telephone and call an existing client for breakfast, lunch or dinner? Think about how many salespeople miss out on opportunities to sit down and continue the relationship-building process with their patrons and, during the process, learn of other potential opportunities as well."

That conversation really started my wheels turning. You should make it a priority to carve out time on a regular basis to sit down and share a meal with existing customers. Explain to them that you are first, following up to be certain they are satisfied with your product or service and second, looking for ways to expand your business. Be honest and forthcoming with your intentions. Once they understand what you are trying to accomplish, most will respect your sincerity and assist if possible, while one or two might not be in a position to help.

Don't shy away from these opportunities to ask for assistance. Take into account that these are the individuals who sing your praises and share their experiences about you and what you tout with the rest of the world. However, it is important to remember not to overuse or abuse this privilege.

69

Most importantly, never forget that existing clients are not just current but also potential customers. Make it a priority to listen to the needs and wants of this important group. If you are able to anticipate their needs, devise timely solutions and provide proven results, existing patrons can be a constant source of repeat business.

## Accessible resources

Leads are all around you. No matter what the business, accessible resources are available for all sales representatives committed to building their core customer bases.

What sources exist to help you find that great wealth of leads? As mentioned previously, your network is a great start. In addition to the boundless opportunities we've already explored, listed below are a few well worth your time and attention. If you take the occasion to investigate each one thoroughly, your client base and success rate will increase:

- Referrals from friends and family
- Industry-specific trade shows
- Trade publications and magazines
- Websites
- Database marketing lists
- Charitable events
- Cold call canvassing
- Community gatherings and festivals
- Newspaper articles
- Yellow Pages
- Chamber of Commerce members
- Association member rosters
- Civic club members

Generating new business leads will always be a significant part of sales. Don't ever underestimate the importance of approaching existing clients who are willing to supply names of potential buyers as well as past customers who might be interested in revisiting your product or service. These two suggestions, along with identifying effective accessible resources, will have an enormous influence on your business.

Now that you have invested time, resources and energy in researching who is most likely to purchase from you, the next step is to go out there and meet with them face-to-face. Rub elbows and shake hands with those who, in the very near future, might become your best customers.

## CALL TO ACTION

Throughout the next quarter, share a meal with a handful of existing customers, gauging their satisfaction and exploring new opportunities.

Before the end of the week, create a list of previous clients you are comfortable reconnecting with. Make contact with each one asking for new business.

Generate a list of new business leads from three accessible resources. Then schedule time to contact each prospect.

# 9

## Why Some Say "Yes" and Others Say "No"

Thus far, much emphasis has been placed on habits such as being passionate, well prepared and confident in the product or service you are aligned with. Regardless of your industry, striving to strengthen and expand your business can be extremely rewarding, yet daunting all at the same time.

At the beginning of the day, most salespeople will greet a client prepared with accurate knowledge of a product or service and the tools needed to sell and promote—leading to the assumption that the sales professional knows what to sell.

Understanding what to sell is simply not enough. You must be well versed in the intellectual side of how to sell as well. The typical sales representative works in an environment of incredible stress, great expectations and regular rejection. Statistics show that failure occurs over 70% of the time. Nonetheless, those sales professionals hitting their marks consistently understand the emotional side of their prospects and the processes they go through when choosing to say "yes" instead of saying "no."

## *Why some say "yes"*

When strengthening and expanding your business, it is wise to recognize that each prospect buys for various reasons. Some consumers are motivated to buy because they want the latest and greatest—the key word being *want*; others have a need to acquire a certain type of product or service—the key word being *need*; and some are prone to purchase based on *status*, *impulse* or *peace of mind*.

Whatever the case, it is important to understand the rationalization behind the buyer's potential purchase. These motives are commonly referred to as triggers—ideas that prompt the customer to buy.

*Want* **trigger**: To feel a strong urge or desire for something. There are many instances of purchases based on want. Perhaps you have a favorite band that has just released a new CD, or maybe you collect autographed baseballs and one signed by Mickey Mantle just went on the auction block. These types of purchases are driven by an individual's sense of fulfillment and are often considered luxuries.

*Need* **trigger**: Something that is a requirement or a perceived necessity. When a purchase is made based on need, more specific requirements can usually be identified. For instance, suppose you are a member of a regional association, responsible for coordinating the upcoming annual conference. Included in your duties is securing the keynote speaker. This is a defined need, something essential to the success of the conference. In making the selection, you have a clear objective and a gap to be filled.

*Status* **trigger**: The relative position or standing of somebody or something in a society or other group. Let's face it, no one likes to acknowledge the impact ego has on the decision to buy. Still, look no further than the nearest designer boutique or haberdashery to realize that making a purchase based on the feeling of increased status drives more than one industry around the globe. I'd be willing to wager that status purchases account for more arguments between parents and their children than anything else when it comes to spending hard-earned money.

*Impulse* **trigger**: A sudden wish or urge that prompts an unplanned act. Have you ever thought about the assortment of items surrounding you in the checkout lane of the grocery store? Usually it's a pretty odd assortment of goods. The smart merchandiser knows that products placed closest to the entrance and exit of an establishment are most likely to be scooped up on impulse, thought about only after being seen by the consumer. Don't be fooled into thinking the impulse trigger only applies to add-on sales. Potential customers may begin their search looking for one type of product or service but come away with a totally different selection after following their impulse down an alternate path.

75

*Peace of mind* **trigger**: The state or feeling of being safe, secure and protected. There are many ways this trigger plays into a purchase. Perhaps the stovetop range you own works just fine, but it has been around a few years and you would just feel better replacing it. After all, the neighbor's range caught fire last week due to faulty wiring and caused quite a mess in their kitchen. Although it's not yet necessary, you buy a new range for your own peace of mind.

These illustrations are fairly simple; nevertheless, you can easily equate each trigger to your own experiences as a salesperson, and in doing so use them to your advantage.

No matter what the justification, as a successful sales representative your number one priority is to make sure the patron is completely and unequivocally satisfied at the end of the day. To do this, look for and recognize the trigger or triggers that are vitally important to those you do business with. In the meantime, never underestimate the appreciation customers have when they see that you have put forth the effort to customize your approach to meet their specific needs and expectations.

Tailor your sales presentation, modify your collateral pieces, and throw away your current form proposal letter and design a new one that speaks to the various triggers of your customers. If you feel as though you can improve in relating to your client, then don't let another hour pass doing the same old thing. As the esteemed businessman Max De Pree once said, "We cannot become what we need to be by remaining what we are."

Whatever the trigger that prompts the purchase, successful sales professionals understand that while that emotion may be the starting point, it is by no means the only circumstance leading the customer to their products or services.

## Why some say "no"

76

At the beginning of this book, it was stated that the thought of being turned down tops the list of fears by many. In spite of the situation, any time a customer utters the word "no," disappointment is likely to surface.

So, what are the reasons why some choose not to purchase your product or service? In most cases, there are five possible explanations.

**Financial position:** Oftentimes money is the leading reason why a customer chooses not to complete a transaction. Even though some will willingly express their current standing, most will never let on that finances are an issue.

**Indecision:** It happens frequently—an individual is unable to reach a decision due to the uncertainty of the results. Much time and consideration may be given to a particular product or service, yet for whatever reason that person just can't commit.

**Procrastination:** An existing or potential customer might have good intentions, but putting a purchase off until a later date is always an option just a stone's throw away. If the buyer is not ready to say "yes" but also doesn't rule out the answer "no," it may be a simple case of postponing decision-making.

**Insecurity:** Just as the confidence level of a salesperson impacts the end result, a buyer is no different. Belief or confidence in your product or service affects what the final outcome will be. If the potential customer feels a sense of awkwardness or is uncomfortable with the thought of the purchase, chances are the transaction will not occur.

**Never clearly asked:** This may seldom happen, but when it does it is quite noticeable. Customers must clearly be asked for their business; if not, odds are they will go elsewhere. No matter the pitch, be crystal clear in what you are requesting.

## Negotiate a positive outcome

One of the most challenging and uncomfortable situations you will encounter as a sales representative is the need to negotiate your price. In some instances, you may not have authority or flexibility when it comes to offering a discount. If that is the case, follow your company's policy and develop a kind, respectful response that applies to your situation. Alternately, if you are in a position to negotiate, there are a few simple ideas to keep in mind in order to lessen the stress throughout the process.

**Know what your top, middle and bottom prices are.** Having these pre-set limits and then standing behind them guarantees that you won't be swayed into a poor business decision.

**Utilize the negotiating tool of silence.** Allow your offer to stand on its own merit, and give the prospect a chance to recognize the value for the price quoted.

**Treat all clients equally.** Offering special pricing as a "favor" to a friend can hurt you and call your integrity into question. Your longevity and reputation depend on your clientele's belief that all customers are treated fairly and without bias. If you're trying to build a career as a sales representative, once again keep in mind that it is not a sprint, but a marathon. Outstanding integrity and fairness create goodwill that is priceless.

When the time comes to negotiate, the following situations may very well apply:

- Above all, you want to close this transaction.
- Business is slow, and you need this transaction.
- You suspect that the price of your product or service is too high.

In these types of situations, it is crucial to pledge to remain true to your pre-set limits. Many sales professionals are afraid to stand behind their price because of the mistaken assumption that if they refuse to negotiate, they'll lose their customer. The reality is just the opposite. If you aren't prepared to justify the price of your product or service, your customers will lose respect for both you and what you offer.

**Never apologize for your price, instead present it with confidence.** If you want your prospect to believe the proposed investment presents a good value, you must believe it first. You also have to be willing to walk away when necessary. This demonstrates you are negotiating from a position of strength, and the likely buyer will often conclude that your product or service is worth what you are asking. Your willingness to walk away from a sale comes from the confidence of having other potential clients waiting in the wings. When pressed, never assume a defensive tone. The customer will recognize it immediately, casting doubt on both you and what you offer.

In many instances, your prospect may come to you with a quote from a competitor, asking you to match the price. This can present a different type of negotiating dilemma. It's imperative to do your homework before engaging in this type of negotiation.

**Be certain that if you are competing against another quote, your prospect is comparing apples to apples.** Apart from the amount of knowledge you have about your own product or service, you must have adequate information about your competitor's prior to negotiating a lowered price. Is the value the same? Are the features and benefits comparable? Don't be in a rush to lower your prices until you have done your research.

Customer price objections can be very enticing. You want the sale and the client is offering you an easy way to close it: offer a discount. However, closing a sale means nothing if it is not profitable. Your objective is to create a satisfied customer, consummating a transaction that is profitable for you both.

The ideas that move a potential client to purchase or not are as individual as the customer. Often overlooked, take into account that other reasons might influence the customer's conclusion or determination about your product or service. There is one basic mannerism that you, as the sales representative, have total control over: the expressions you use.

## *Inviting and irritating phrases*

It would have been easy to end this chapter without incorporating this last section; still, it is important to make mention of the casual phrases you

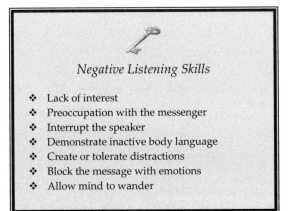

*Negative Listening Skills*

❖ Lack of interest
❖ Preoccupation with the messenger
❖ Interrupt the speaker
❖ Demonstrate inactive body language
❖ Create or tolerate distractions
❖ Block the message with emotions
❖ Allow mind to wander

might speak to existing or potential customers and their impact on the end result.

No matter whether you have been on a sales call with a colleague or were on the other side of the table as a consumer, there is no doubt you've heard expressions that were either inviting or irritating. These strings of words can encourage or discourage a positive conclusion. For instance, I can recall the first time I ever walked onto a car lot by myself. I was eighteen and completely determined to find a truck I liked. I'd never been through the process of purchasing a vehicle before, so my expectations were halfway between certainty and uncertainty of the final outcome.

"Hey partner, what can I show you today?" were the first words that came out of the mouth of the salesman as he walked across the lot. For the next forty minutes or so, if I could have had a dollar for every time I was addressed as "Hey partner" I would have had enough to pay for my sales tax right then and there.

Maybe it was my age, or perhaps it was the expression on my face as I browsed the lot for that perfect ride. Whatever it was that gave the salesperson the impression that I was his "partner" was totally wrong. Not only was it irritating, it made the entire process awkward. I did not

80

buy a truck that day—not solely because of the phrase that was constantly used in addressing me, but it sure didn't help.

It is an easy thing to do: Create a two, three or four word phrase and begin using it around everyone. Always be aware—phrases are interpreted in many different ways. I'm sure I was not the first or last person this sales representative used "Hey partner" with, but I can guarantee you I wasn't the only one who took issue with it. Be aware of the unique phrases you develop and use in your own communication patterns.

| INVITING PHRASES | IRRITATING PHRASES |
|---|---|
| Thank you. | I don't make the rules. |
| May I have your permission? | You don't understand. |
| I apologize for your inconvenience. | I'll tell you what. |
| It's a pleasure meeting you. | I'm helping someone else right now. |
| You are very kind. | Here you go, honey. |
| It's a privilege to work with you. | It's not my job. |
| I would appreciate the opportunity. | Let me put you on hold. |
| I appreciate your time and consideration. | Have you made up your mind yet? |

There will always be motivating factors behind why some say "yes" while others say "no." At times, the psychology that plays into a customer's buying pattern can be easily understood, or leave you quite confused. Either way, draw on the explanations shared in this chapter and remember you should always try not to take others' opposition personally. As long as you continue offering a sound product or service and make the effort to consistently understand the emotional side of the prospect, you will obtain your own peace of mind.

## ∽ CALL TO ACTION ∼

Look back over your last ten sales and identify the triggers that moved the customer to say "yes." Recall your own response and interaction with each, and look for ways to apply your proven techniques to current prospects.

Review the last five sales you've lost and explore why each prospect turned you down. If you have not already started keeping track of the reasons potential customers have said "no," now is the time to begin.

Over the course of the next week, make a conscious effort to listen to yourself when speaking to others. See if you can identify phrases that could possibly be irritating.

# 10

## ARRANGE A STURDY FRAMEWORK

No matter what product or service you are selling, the framework of your sales process should always be sturdy. The stronger you construct your frame, the better the likelihood that you will experience positive results. If you are scattered in the execution of your process, odds are, your success rate will be hit or miss.

When structuring your individual sales routine, be aware that there are three points crucial to arranging a strong framework. Let's take a closer look at these all-important pillars.

### Pillar One — Hone an Effective Approach

Not long ago my colleagues and I decided to stop at a good old-fashioned Southern barbecue restaurant. Now if you're like me, when your stomach is begging for attention, all barbecue tastes the same—so it doesn't take much to impress you. This particular dining experience was a bit different, though.

It wasn't the aroma swirling in the air from the beef brisket, chopped pork and roasted chicken, or the ribs steadily sizzling above the pit. The décor was appealing, but nothing I hadn't seen before.

What made this evening different was an approach that turned out to be extremely effective.

"Hey y'all, my name's Sally," our server said with a big grin while passing my colleagues and me menus. "Have y'all ever been here before?"

During the course of what I considered to be a very welcoming introduction, our waitress pulled a chair up to the table and proceeded to answer questions we had about the various items on the menu—from cooking techniques to seasonings to sauces—nothing was left out.

Since this was my first visit to the restaurant, I found the information to be very accommodating and presented in a non-intrusive way. If I wasn't impressed at that point, what happened next sealed the deal.

In between attending to other diners and before bringing out our orders, Sally brought us a complimentary plate of fried potatoes and a half-dozen different types of barbecue sauce.

"Since y'all have never tasted our sauces before, let me give you a little taste tour," she said while introducing us to flavors bottled with names like Georgia's Mustard, Texas Pit, Sweet and Zesty, and Devil's Spit.

I will never forget thinking, "Wow, Sally really seems to enjoy her work and in turn does a great job serving customers. Her approach is sincere, not pushy. The knowledge she shares is accurate and very useful—and this really helps, especially when your stomach is turning front flips."

Looking back, I must say the entire dining experience was a hit. Not once did our glasses of sweet tea go dry, nor did that enthusiastic smile ever leave Sally's face. The approach she used from the minute we were welcomed to her table until we got up to leave was fun and memorable.

Let me be clear: The food was good that night, and each and every other time I've revisited the establishment. All the same, that's not why I return. I go back because of how I was treated—not only as a customer, but as an individual who truly mattered.

## Whatever your approach, be genuine

Let's concentrate for a moment on this significant first pillar. Is your approach sincere? Have clear objectives been established? What outcome are you working toward? Is the entire process memorable? These and many other questions should be asked when pondering the initial contact you have with a potential customer.

85

**Being genuine and sincere toward others breeds trust and confidence**. From the moment our server walked up to the table, her attitude radiated authentic interest in us.

**Defining clear objectives helps keep you on target while breathing self-assurance into your approach.** When my colleagues and I had questions about a particular menu item, our server was there to provide the answers. After she initially welcomed us, it was evident this was one of her objectives. Another noticeable intention was to make us feel as comfortable as possible. That was apparent when she pulled up a chair and treated us like family.

**What are you hoping transpires as a result of your approach?** In the case of our server, two things were clear. First, she was working extremely hard to earn a good tip. Second, I'm sure her aim was to give each of us a good enough reason to return again. Thanks to her method, she achieved both. Not only did I tip her well, each time I return to eat barbecue I ask to be seated in her section—not just because she worked hard, but because her work was genuine.

**Regardless of how much time you have in front of a prospective client, make your approach worth remembering.** I must say, to this day I have never had any other server take the time to introduce me to a number of different options as part of a taste tour. Sally's style was original and well worth remembering.

While this was a simple dining experience, it serves as a powerful example of only getting one chance to present an effective approach. Remember, as long as you stay true to yourself, your approach will be genuine.

In a world today where there is much insincerity, isn't it a breath of fresh air when you find someone's approach to be authentic, not artificial? Yours can be truly noticeable and, at the end of the day, have a gigantic effect on the success or failure of selling your product or service. When perfecting your method, consider who or what may be your initial point of contact. Let's first reflect on the gatekeeper.

## *Your approach with the gatekeeper*

When calling on new business, you and I both know the chances of speaking directly to a decision-maker on the first call are slim to none. Odds are you will encounter an assistant on the other end of the line or be transferred to voice mail. Regardless of who or what picks up, the responsibility of expressing the most effective approach possible rests on your shoulders. Let me explain just how crucial this point really is.

Whether you find yourself speaking to an administrative assistant, receptionist, switchboard operator or secretary, make sure you give that individual your utmost respect. This applies not only when you are on the telephone but when you are in person as well. The gatekeeper holds the key to the door you are trying to enter.

This intermediary is vitally important to reaching the decision-maker. An assistant could approach the boss and say, "You should speak to this gentleman...he has a product I think could really help our company." On the flip side, the gatekeeper might state, "This guy wants you to call him back. I don't know what he wants, but I believe he is trying to sell you something...oh, by the way, he was extremely rude."

Most individuals in decision-making roles listen closely to their assistants. As a sales professional, make it a habit to show respect to all gatekeepers and understand that you must convince them that what you have to say is of enough importance to take their bosses' time. If you talk down to them, act impatient or become impolite, 99 times out of 100 you will not gain entrance through the gate.

On the other hand, if you approach the intermediary with sincerity, outline clear objectives for wanting to speak to the boss, explain how the outcome of the meeting can be beneficial to the organization and make the conversation memorable through your enthusiasm, odds are good that the outcome will be positive.

Some sales professionals follow all the right rules and still don't get through the door. This often leaves them asking themselves, "What do I need to do differently?" Here are five questions worth considering to raise your success rate:

**When speaking with the gatekeeper, am I appealing to a large enough need to justify a meeting with the boss?** Remember how important satisfying needs are in the arena of sales.

**When speaking with the gatekeeper, am I appealing to a sense of responsibility to put me through if what I want to discuss is important enough to impose on the boss's time, in the gatekeeper's opinion?** Keep in mind, the intermediary is always on the lookout for unwanted intrusions on your prospect's time.

**If you have determined you are not getting through to the decision-maker at this point, do you ask the gatekeeper for a suggested time to call back?** Many salespeople make the mistake of just saying, "I'll call back," instead of attempting to set up an appointment to ensure the prospect's availability.

**When you call back, do you address the gatekeeper by name, referring to your last conversation and pointing out you followed the suggestion to call at the appointed time?** In most instances, the intermediary will try to connect you with the potential prospect if politely reminded of the recommendation.

**After leaving several messages for a decision-maker, do you make it a point to schedule an office visit where you can meet the gatekeeper face-to-face?** It is very difficult for an intermediary to turn down your in-person request for a future appointment with the boss.

If you utilize the proper approach, the gatekeeper can become your best inroad when trying to connect with your prospective client. Bear in mind, the human element is only one part of the equation when trying to get your foot in the door.

For anyone who makes a multitude of calls on a daily basis, leaving voice messages is nothing new. In fact, with the prevalence of Caller ID and voice mail, the entire business landscape has changed. If you are telephoning a new prospect and your number isn't recognized, odds are your call will be routed to voice mail.

Nonetheless, there are several things to keep in mind when interacting with these electronic gatekeepers. I touched on a few of these ideas when discussing your own voice messaging system in an earlier chapter; now let's take a more in-depth look at what should be considered when calling others:

- Speak slowly and directly into the mouthpiece of the telephone.
- Leave your name and number twice—at the beginning and end of your message.
- Leave a brief but complete message as to why you are calling.
- Use a friendly and respectful tone of voice.

**Example:** *"Hello, Mr. Smith. My name is (your name) with (company name). My telephone number is (number). Realizing how busy you are, I will only take a moment of your time. I'm a professional trainer who presents sales and customer service seminars to companies around the globe. Many organizations have found the content I share to be of great value. At your convenience, I would like to visit with you by telephone to request permission to forward information detailing the benefits of my services. Would you please return my call at (number)? Or, I will be happy to follow up with you in the next day or two. Once again, my name is (your name). I look forward to speaking with you soon."*

89

After leaving a message such as this, be prepared to call again and leave a different voice message that builds on the same thought process. Keep in mind leaving a voice message may be your first and only chance to impact a potential client. Craft one that portrays you in the best possible light.

Occasionally, the first point of communication with a potential customer will occur through the gatekeeper we know as the Internet, specifically electronic mail. This requires that additional attention be given to honing your e-mail approach.

Follow the same basic rules previously listed for voice mails, with one noticeable exception. Due to the fact that you will be presenting your prospect with indisputable, written communication, take special care to not only verify the information included, but to check grammar, sentence structure, spelling and etiquette. Much like words spoken, once sent, an e-mail usually can't be retrieved. Put your best approach forward when utilizing this delicate form of communication.

## Your approach with the decision-maker

Never is your approach more important than when finally connecting with the decision-maker. Authenticity, sincerity and honesty will carry you further than any selling point offered. True, you may have the latest and greatest product or service with a price that beats all of your competitors. However, without a memorable approach, you will likely be just another salesperson touting yet one more commodity.

90

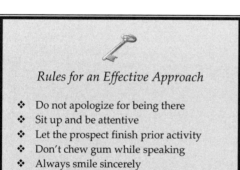

*Rules for an Effective Approach*

- ❖ Do not apologize for being there
- ❖ Sit up and be attentive
- ❖ Let the prospect finish prior activity
- ❖ Don't chew gum while speaking
- ❖ Always smile sincerely
- ❖ Pronounce the prospect's name properly
- ❖ Don't be too clever or common

The method you master that targets your face-to-face encounter with a potential client is the basis for not only your initial, but all subsequent sales calls with that individual. Your ability to establish a relationship built on rapport and trust, ultimately leading to the conversion of the prospect into a long-term patron, is grounded in your authentic, effective approach. A tremendous amount of study, reflection and practice are needed to accurately compose the technique that you tailor with your customer in mind. Synonymous with product or service identification, it can accurately be stated that your ultimate, polished style will define you, the sales representative, to your customers.

## Pillar Two — Seven Steps to a Successful Sales Call

After obtaining permission to make your pitch, the successful sales call is broken up into seven important steps. By mastering these ideas and remaining consistent in utilizing them, you will find a steady level of comfort and confidence when presenting your product or service to both existing and potential customers, whether in person or over the telephone.

*Step One: Prepare in advance* — Arranging your sales call in advance will increase the likelihood that the visit with your potential client will unfold in a seamless manner. You will be ready for any curves that may come your way, and the end result will be poise and professionalism.

Prepare in such a way to ensure the presentation flows in a logical order. Don't cut corners or condense critical information. Determine what supporting materials will be used and what leave-behind collateral will be utilized.

91

Once you have developed your pitch, conduct a dress rehearsal. It is always smart to practice your delivery prior to making personal contact with the prospect. During this process, consider any objections you think you might receive, and make sure you have legitimate responses.

*Step Two: Introduction* — Every sales call begins with the opportunity to provide an enthusiastic introduction. It is the launching pad that can open the door wide or merely push it ajar. The objective throughout your introduction is to create a level of comfort and familiarity, expand the rapport initiated during your approach, and earn the prospect's confidence and trust. Script a pleasant introduction that not only includes a warm greeting, but gives pertinent information about yourself and your company. Remember the basics: Be neat, professional, relaxed, friendly and confident. Most importantly—smile, smile, smile!

_Step Three: Opening statement_ — This is your opportunity to grab the attention and interest of the person you're visiting and create excitement about what you have to sell. If your opening statement falls flat, your prospect's mind will move on to something else or pay minimal attention to what you have to say. There are several common, easy to use, attention-getting techniques that can be used to prepare valuable opening statements:

- _Satisfy curiosity._ This type of opening statement appeals to the potential client's sense of curiosity. The prospect is instinctively anxious to hear what you have to say in order to satisfy the urge to know more. **Example:** "Ms. Moore, I am here to discuss your technological advances. I'm sure that you want to remain on the cutting edge of inventory control. Have you heard about our Information at Your Fingertips mobile inventory system?"

- _Demonstrate benefits._ Giving the potential client an outline of the advantages your product or service offers is a definite way of opening the dialogue for further discussion. **Example:** "Ms. Moore, I'm here to talk about streamlining your inventory accounting system. With the demands on your daily schedule, I'm sure you want to work with a method that is accurate and trouble-free. Our Information at Your Fingertips mobile inventory system will take the worries out of losing a customer if the product isn't on your sales floor."

- _At your assistance._ With the daily demands on schedules, your prospect may be taxed not only by responsibilities, but overwhelmed at the idea of one more decision that has to be made after hearing your pitch. Positioning yourself as someone who gives assistance is often the best way to gain the potential client's trust and acceptance of your product or service. **Example:** "Ms. Moore, to help save you some time, may I show you a technique for immediate on-the-floor

92

inventory accountability and assist you in training your staff on increasing sales using our system?"

*Step Four: Questioning period* — Ask numerous, specific questions to continue building rapport and showcasing your listening skills. Learning not only to ask pertinent questions, but to listen for insightful answers is a multifaceted skill that is acquired through practice and experience. Use this period to build the prospect's interest, determine needs, and establish the niche where your product or service will fit.

Questioning the prospect is designed to uncover your potential client's needs. These needs include those of the prospect's organization, its customers, its employees and the individual with whom you are having the dialogue. Skillful questioning is valuable not only during the sales call, but critical to overall success in selling.

93

An easy way to visualize the order of the questioning process is to remember the three "F's":

- **Fact** — When qualifying a potential customer, get as many facts as possible about the business.
- **Focus** — Focus in on the greatest possibilities your product or service has in relation to the prospect's needs.
- **Feelings** — Recognize the potential client's feelings and acknowledge their importance to the overall sales process from start to finish.

Throughout the questioning period, remember: The most important skill for you as a salesperson to perfect—and the one that will assist the questioning process in the most comfortable, natural manner—is simply to listen. As you become skilled in knowing what to ask and the way to ask it, you will be able to fully concentrate on the answers and not the questions.

What follows are five techniques that will strengthen your questioning and listening skills. As you will see, the purpose for mastering each skill weighs heavily in favor of increased success during your sales pitch.

| TECHNIQUE/SKILL | PURPOSE |
|---|---|
| **Paraphrase** — Restate in your own words what you think the other person just said. | • Allows the speaker to make sure you understand<br>• Corrects misinterpretation |
| **Check perception** — Describe what you perceive to be the other person's feelings in order to check your understanding. | • Communicates listener's willingness to understand the speaker as a person<br>• Allows the speaker to confirm or correct the listener's perception |
| **Empathize** — State that you can understand the reason for what was said. | • Shows you are listening<br>• Strongly encourages the person to continue talking about the idea |
| **Confirm** — Restate almost exactly what has just been said to demonstrate your understanding. | • Allows the speaker to hear what you heard<br>• Encourages the speaker to re-examine what was said |
| **Encourage** — Use phrases that encourage the speaker to continue or open up. | • Communicates the listener's interest and desire to hear more |

94

Questioning should continue to build the prospect's interest in your product or service. Ask questions with enthusiasm, showing interest through your voice, facial expressions and body language. Once you have all the information you need to give an effective presentation, the questioning period is complete.

*Step Five: Presentation* — You are now ready to present information on your product or service for the potential client's consideration. Presentations need to be understandable, interesting, believable and persuasive in order to effectively demonstrate benefits to the prospect.

As you begin, reiterate your gratitude for being given the opportunity to present your pitch. Whether you are given five minutes or fifty, your potential client's time is valuable and acknowledging this fact will be appreciated. Exhibiting humility and appreciation on your end will help the prospect relax and be more open to what you have to sell.

Set the scene for what you are about to pitch. A major point to recognize is that while your overall framework should not only be sturdy and consistent, each presentation needs to be tailored to the individual prospect. It should address the needs, wants and benefits determined during the questioning period. Communicate information that will let the potential client know you have done your research and have identified a fit for what you have to offer.

Once you have painted a clear picture, begin presenting an overview. You may wish to briefly list items of supporting collateral that will be left behind for later review before diving into the specifics regarding your product or service. Give the high points and most important characteristics, while leaving room for the prospect to be inventive in recognizing ways to utilize your product or service according to perceived needs. Remember to keep it simple. Don't take thirty minutes to tell your story if it can be told in fifteen.

Allow your potential customer to be your captive audience, while at the same time remaining one yourself. Listen to the comments and, if possible, work them into functional ideas during the presentation. As you do this, focus on the prospect, not the product or service. Relate the presentation to the situation, using tangible comparisons. One way to do this is to construct sentences using the potential client as the subject and your product or service as the object. For example: "Ms. Moore, your customers will appreciate the speed with which our mobile inventory system gives your salesperson stock information."

Your reputation and that of your product or service are crucial to cementing the validity of what you can provide to the prospect. Present the names of several clients you've done business with and offer letters of reference for the potential customer's inspection. Oftentimes, the opinion of someone who is in a similar position will hold more weight with the prospect than anything you as a salesperson can say. While remaining humble and matter-of-fact, let your reputation and that of your product or service speak for themselves.

Once you have provided a good representation of your offering, now is the time to detail the investment you wish the client to make. Help the prospect understand what the cost entails and what additional perks or incentives you can offer beyond the obvious. Presenting your product or service as a beneficial element to the prospect's business, while encouraging ownership through investment, brings your offering to a personal level and motivates the client toward a favorable closing.

Be prepared to respond to queries and hesitations regarding your product or service's cost to your potential customer. No one ever offers more than the asking price; quite the contrary, most will try to negotiate a discount or reduction in fee. Have full knowledge of and permission for whatever concessions you can make, if any, and never promise the client anything you can't deliver. This applies not only to cost, but also to what you are providing in the final exchange.

To summarize, become adept at giving presentations by embracing a consistent process. Give your pitch in the same sequence each time, and practice it frequently in order to stay in tune with what you are re-presenting. Tailor each section of the presentation to your prospect's specific needs. Include as many benefits as you can throughout your pitch, paying special attention to the particular niche you have targeted. As you work through your presentation, be attuned to the potential client's stages of interest and omit features that are met with disinterest by the prospect.

Following this template for each successive sales call will not only help your presentations feel comfortable to you, they will go more smoothly overall. Certainly you will want to make adjustments as the need arises. If you discover something additional that will be of assistance in making your presentation, by all means test its effectiveness and adjust accordingly. Accommodating the prospect and exercising flexibility while remaining strong in your method will contribute greatly to your sales success.

_Step Six: Closing_ — You have given a strong pitch, established good rapport and piqued the interest of your potential client. Now is the time to make an unforgettable argument that can influence your prospect to purchase from you. Your memorable closing should be comprised of the following three steps:

- **Summarize the benefits of your product or service** — Recapping your offer while stressing the benefits to the client will assist the customer in making a decision.
- **Request a commitment** — Utilize a defined call to action: "You might like this, you ought to try it."
- **Be quiet and listen** — The client may have some last-minute questions or concerns; take the chance to understand them and put them to rest.

Use positive language while presenting your memorable closing. Assume that the attitude of agreement has been reached. Don't be nervous or uncomfortable and show no doubt or hesitancy.

There are several techniques a successful sales professional should be familiar with and master when closing a presentation.

_Close on an objection._ This comes at a point where you have isolated one final objection. The actual close comes through the promise to buy if the objection can be overcome. For example: "It looks like the only thing standing between us is the training schedule for the mobile inventory system. If the schedule can be rearranged, may I write up the needed units?"

*Narrative close.* This is a summary of benefits that ends in a question asking for commitment. For example: "Let me review the model needed for your inventory requirements. The system should accommodate a thirteen-digit item number and be able to be upgraded to a bar code system at a later date. May I have your commitment for two units given these specifications?"

*Ask for the order close.* Simply ask the prospect to complete the transaction. For example: "Ms. Moore, have we covered everything?" (Yes) "May I place the order for two mobile inventory system units?"

*Extra incentive close.* Offer incentives for closing now or on your terms. For example: "Ms. Moore, we will provide you with free software and upgrades for twelve months if you confirm the order today. Is that acceptable?"

*Impending event close.* This close urges prospects to act now because there is no time to waste. For example: "Due to increased demand for inventory control, we typically sell out of this system during the holiday season. Could I go ahead and process your order today?"

*Assumptive close.* This technique asks an indirect question based on the assumption that an agreement has been reached. For example: "Ms. Moore, since we seem to be in agreement, may I go ahead and send your inventory system units out?"

Though each of the above techniques is effective as well as easy to use, develop your own repertoire of closes, incorporating the methods that both fit your situation and that you are most comfortable with. Memorize and practice them, and they will become second nature to you.

---

*Seven Strategies for a Powerful Closing*

❖ Always close
❖ Use positive language
❖ Be persistent and sincere
❖ Keep a strong point in reserve
❖ Use the three-step process to close
❖ Look for buyer signals to determine when to close
❖ Avoid alternatives after the prospect has agreed

---

*Step Seven: Feedback* — Once you have closed, you will have the opportunity to answer questions and handle objections. Be factual and unbiased with your answers, making sure not to become defensive or allow emotion to enter into the exchange.

99

Don't give long-winded responses that do everything but address the questions. In the unlikely event you are unsure of a correct reply, acknowledge this to your prospect, give assurance that you will gather the information immediately and then make good on your promise. At the conclusion of the feedback period, if questions remain unanswered, telephone anyone necessary to obtain the needed answers. Be sure not to let this situation rattle you; exhibit poise and confidence throughout, and you will retain your potential client's trust and respect.

Asking for additional feedback from the prospective client will not only help you improve, have a higher close rate and cement your relationship with the prospect, it will be your point of difference. The obvious questions are: "What have I not provided for you?" and "How can I better assist you?" A few more you might consider are: "Have I targeted your goals and objectives?" "Would you like to share any constructive criticism with me?"

"Has our product or service met your expectations?" "Is there anything else I can do to make your job easier?"

Don't be afraid to learn from your prospect. You can be self-confident while exercising humility in your quest for excellence.

## Pillar Three — Persist in Your Follow-Through

"If you say you're going to do it...then do it!" This simple statement has been drilled into the minds of salespeople since the beginning of time. Nevertheless, overextended schedules, everyday distractions and one meeting right after the next make such a simple idea quite difficult to enact.

If you are searching for that one point of difference in your sales routine that will help you achieve favorable results, look no further. Without any doubt, the best way to distinguish yourself from your competition while building long-lasting relationships is to follow through with your existing and potential clients—not just every now and then, but all the time. As elementary as it might sound, in many cases the vast majority of sales professionals has not perfected this habit.

We have all been on both sides of the fence. Somebody wants to introduce you to a great product. Every reason is shared why you should buy right then and there. For whatever reason you're hesitant, but that's "not a problem" because you are promised a call back. Even though you choose not to make the purchase on the spot, you are still interested. So, a couple of days pass—then a week, and two more. The follow-up you were assured never transpired. Did that impact your decision to buy? Well, naturally it did. Not only did it influence your impression of the product, it most likely affected your perception of the individual selling it as well.

This scenario is nothing new. Odds are we all have given our word at some point and then for whatever reason dropped the ball. We are only human, right? Correct, but only you and I control how many times the ball slips through our hands. I can't think of many things patrons appreciate more than experiencing the results delivered by a sales professional keeping a promise.

## Control the tempo

Any type of correspondence—whether handwritten, electronic or verbal—sets a tempo for the recipient. The timing of its delivery is no different. When a potential customer requests information about your product or service, forwarding the materials in a timely manner greatly increases your chance of success. It is no secret that it costs less to do business with a satisfied client than to constantly be prospecting for new ones. With this in mind, the motivation for being prompt and consistent is evident.

It is easy to assume that once the materials have been sent, the prospect will take over from there. In some cases this may be true, yet more times than not, persisting in your follow-through is what closes the sale. Placing courtesy phone calls, sending follow-up e-mails and dropping handwritten notes, along with other simple actions, help create a positive tempo between you and the existing or potential customer.

101

Over the years, sales and marketing research have indicated that it takes nine impressions to make an initial sale and six impressions in a year to maintain top-of-mind awareness. You should definitely put a system in place that makes it possible to reach out at the very minimum of four times a year to existing and potential customers.

An impression can be presented in many different ways: standard letter, voice message, e-mail blast, brochure, electronic newsletter, news clipping or a personal phone call. Your sales cycle will determine how many impressions it takes to make the sale. Your continued follow-up after the sale dictates how long the relationship between you and the client lasts.

## *Follow-through practices*

**Handwritten notes:** Not long ago, I was in a position to hire a new employee. After sorting through various applications, a colleague and I narrowed the pool down to sixteen prospective employees. Interviews were scheduled for each of them and the process began. After two weeks of meeting with applicants, I was very impressed with more than a few. Several days later, as I was making the final decision, I noticed that only one of the applicants had followed up with a handwritten thank you note. Guess who got the job?

As simple and outdated as it may seem, a thank you note can set you apart, especially in this e-mail savvy world. Granted, the abundance of technology today can make things such as note writing easier, but that doesn't necessarily mean that you should depend on it. Not only is a personal handwritten note polite, it also demonstrates that you value the person to whom you are sending the note. In addition, don't shy away from sending a thank you note to the client's spouse, if applicable. This simple acknowledgment will be greatly appreciated.

It only takes a minute to jot down a note, yet it can open paths for new relationships and opportunities. Aside from this, it will also make you feel better about yourself. A little thanks goes a long way.

**Birthday and holiday cards:** Think about how much "unsolicited mail" you receive on a daily basis. How nice it is to check the mailbox and see a handwritten envelope amidst all of the credit card offers and flyers. Which do you open first? A birthday or holiday card can be the highlight of anyone's day. Stay away from the obvious and stand out from the crowd by choosing a holiday that others may overlook, such as St. Patrick's Day, Memorial Day or Labor Day. Be inventive! If you can't find a card for the holiday you have chosen, you might want to invest in having one made. Your investment will be a timeless reminder of your follow-through.

**Magazine and newspaper clippings:** The first time I ever made the Babe Ruth All-Star team as a young boy, a local bank clipped my photo from the newspaper and sent it to my parents and me with a brief note of congratulations. It left a major impression, one I remember clearly. Clip articles from magazines and newspapers about your client's business or civic involvement and send them along with a note. To make a lasting impression, have the articles laminated with your business card at the bottom.

**Share a favorite book:** Choose a book that holds a special meaning to you. Send copies to clients as a follow-up gift for their patronage. Not only is this a nice gesture, it can also prompt future dialogue that might lead to additional business. Don't forget to write a brief inscription inside the front cover.

**Electronic newsletter:** Create and distribute an electronic newsletter as a way to reach out and follow up with clients. This can be as simple as writing a Word document that contains interesting, timely content; inserting photos or other visually appealing items; and creating a PDF. You can send this via e-mail on a monthly or quarterly basis. A word of caution: Don't overuse this instrument or it will lose its effectiveness.

103

**Work your A.I.L.:** Throughout your sales routine, be certain to create and work your "All Important List" of existing and potential clients. Picking up the telephone and making a two-minute call is a great way to remain friendly and familiar with your patrons. It may also be the reminder they needed to consider doing business with you!

When arranging a sturdy framework for your sales routine, recognize the elements that comprise each of the three pillars presented. The specifics just discussed should serve as your blueprint when constructing the process that is most effective for you. While this section presents tips that will guide you as you fully master the art of salesmanship, let's recap the earlier chapters that—incorporated with your framework as part of your entire sales structure—will assist you in achieving your utmost promise:

- COMMIT TO REACHING YOUR FULL POTENTIAL — Release your knowledge, enthusiasm and passion.
- STRUCTURE THE DAY TO WORK IN YOUR FAVOR — Manage your process with a system that works for you.
- ORGANIZE THE TOOLS YOU DEPEND ON — Inventory the components that comprise your sales arsenal.
- DEVELOP SOUND MENTORS — Succeed through the wisdom of others.
- UNDERSTAND WHAT YOUR NAME IS ATTACHED TO — Build credibility, confidence and trust through your knowledge.
- PUT YOUR RIVALS TO WORK FOR YOU — Expand your strengths by exploring and understanding your competition.
- BE AWARE OF YOUR APPEARANCE — The first impression you make influences your success.
- SEEK OUT NEW BUSINESS LEADS — Make it a priority to search out new business aggressively.
- WHY SOME SAY "YES" AND OTHERS SAY "NO" — Realize some are prone to purchase based on status, impulse or peace of mind.
- ARRANGE A STURDY FRAMEWORK — Establish strong pillars on which to build your success.

## ⟶◦ ONE FINAL CALL TO ACTION ◦⟵

Now is the time to begin selling with confidence. Starting with the first chapter, review each call to action key and unlock your potential. Don't allow this to be just another book you've read and placed on your shelf. Let this resource continue working for you!

# ANSWERS TO FIFTEEN ESSENTIAL QUESTIONS

QUESTION — **What can I do to distinguish myself from others as a successful sales representative?**

ANSWER — Have the right mental attitude and be passionate about what you represent. If you believe wholeheartedly in your product or service, you will be knowledgeable and prepared when pitching to a potential client.

QUESTION — **What practices can assist in creating a sound structure for increased productivity?**

ANSWER — Maintaining physical as well as mental efficiency is a cornerstone of a high producer. By organizing your desk and briefcase, filing system, automobile, calendar, electronic devices and messaging system, you can have full control of crucial areas that will distinguish you as proficient in your field and place you ahead of the competition.

106

QUESTION — **How can I obtain letters of reference from previous clients without seeming egotistical or self-serving?**

ANSWER — Satisfied customers are usually eager to share a positive experience with others. By asking them to support you and the company you represent, you are giving them ownership in your success. Not only does this referral show they made a wise choice, it gives them a feeling of accomplishment knowing they are helping others obtain the same sense of satisfaction and fulfillment they themselves have received. To do this, always ask in a respectful tone of voice, be careful not to apply pressure and be sure to let them know you understand if they are unable to assist you in this process.

QUESTION — **How can I build credibility and confidence in the minds of my customers?**

ANSWER — Complete product knowledge not only builds credibility with your clients but diminishes doubts and increases self-confidence. Fully understanding your product or service offerings is the key to increasing client trust.

QUESTION — **Besides product knowledge, how can I help increase my client's comfort level with what I have to offer?**

ANSWER — Allow existing and prospective customers to see the real you. Sincerity, excitement, a pleasant demeanor and quality care will help your patrons feel more at ease and accept what you have to offer.

QUESTION — **How can my competition help me to become a greater producer?**

ANSWER — Realizing the choices prospective clients have and focusing on what your competition does well allow you to increase your strengths when providing customers a choice. In addition, knowing your rivals' weaknesses allows you to capitalize on what you do better.

107

QUESTION — **What can I do to increase my rebound power?**

ANSWER — First and foremost, don't ever give up! Continue asking for constructive feedback and then implement any suggestions or ideas that you feel will strengthen your pitch. Through this process, you will gain added confidence and rebound at a quicker pace.

QUESTION — **Is my appearance really as important as the features and benefits of my product or service?**

ANSWER — Your appearance sends a message to your customer. It is up to you whether that message is positive or negative. Not only is your personal reputation on display when presenting yourself, it's the storefront for the product or service you represent. Remember, pride of appearance translates to belief in self and what you put forth each day—both personally and professionally.

**QUESTION — Up until now, I have not given much thought to my body language. What steps can I take to improve the way I communicate nonverbally?**

ANSWER — The basics of using body language to your advantage are simple. Always have a warm smile, offer a firm handshake and make good eye contact. Be aware of your posture and carry yourself with dignity, being certain to avoid projecting arrogance or conceit. Use appropriate hand gestures while respecting your client's space. Above all, be aware of your tone of voice and volume as well as your attentiveness to the client.

**QUESTION — Where should I begin looking for mentors?**

ANSWER — Friends and family are always good places to start. In addition, though, search out individuals who have enjoyed sustained success in your particular field. Work on establishing three to four solid relationships that are based on honesty, trust and two-way communication.

**QUESTION — What is the best way to build my client base?**

ANSWER — While there are many ways to find new leads, developing three areas in which you already have inroads will help build your client base quickly. Begin with previous customers. If they have had a positive experience when dealing with you in the past, your job is half done. If their experience left something to be desired, you have a tremendous opportunity to change their opinion. In addition to previous clientele, existing customers can be your best advertisers and referrals. They know your track record and will most likely be willing to share a positive word. Finally, tap into your industry resources as well as standard marketing opportunities to reach new arenas. Not only will you expand your client base, odds are you'll expand your knowledge and horizons as well.

QUESTION — **Is there a rule of thumb for how often I should contact the customers in my database?**

ANSWER — Once a quarter is a good idea. Be creative and thoughtful in the ways you communicate with past, present and potential customers. Remembering clients on their birthdays, sending holiday cards and following up with a telephone call after a purchase are all effective ways of keeping you front and center.

QUESTION — **With the competition today, how can my company and I stand out from the crowd?**

ANSWER — Consistently delivering on your product or service while showing care and concern for your customers' feelings will not only entice them to purchase, it will become your best advertising through their word of mouth. A lasting, positive experience goes far when clients tell their friends and associates about their dealings with you and your company. Hone a unique, sincere approach and you will not only enjoy your job, you'll enjoy repeat business.

QUESTION — **Is emotion a major factor when considering why some customers buy?**

ANSWER — When emotions need soothing, people often reach for something to consume. Though not always recognized for what it is, this concept is mirrored in many impulse shoppers as well as those who purchase methodically. Think about it, how many dozens of roses have been delivered after a disagreement to say "I'm sorry?" The purchaser most likely derived as much comfort and satisfaction from sending the bouquet as the recipient did in receiving them. On both ends of the spectrum, emotions were soothed. With the exception of true, determined need, purchases triggered by want, status, impulse or peace of mind are all born out of emotion.

QUESTION — **How can I continue to enjoy selling my product or service?**

ANSWER — Every once in a while take a deep breath and relax. Recall the things you have accomplished. Be thankful for them and allow that positive energy to lead you down new roads. The imagination you possessed at the beginning of your career still lives within. Unleash it once again and have fun during the process. Stress, tension and ongoing challenges will always arise; how you deal with each of them influences your level of enjoyment.

# THIRTEEN HABITS OF PITCHING WITH CONFIDENCE

# Introduction

A sales representative's ability to communicate a precise point while maintaining the attention of the potential client is a critical skill to obtain in the quest toward success. From eye contact to tone of voice, you have the opportunity to leave a strong impression with each prospect you meet.

While the product or service being pitched is the key element in a presentation, your delivery of the information makes the message succeed with the prospect or fall flat. You must become comfortable with your own unique style; it is up to you to define what works best in your situation and practice until you've mastered your technique.

Most employers are constantly searching for individuals who are not only ambassadors for their products or services, but are adept at delivering an effective presentation with successful end results. Becoming empowered with the habits found in this bonus section will not only serve a great purpose in your sales career today, it will also have a profound effect on other areas of your life for years to come.

As humans, we present on a daily basis through casual conversation. We become comfortable with our vocabularies and the ability to persuade others to embrace our message. The following pages will sharpen the skills you acquired at an early age. They will complement the techniques you are familiar with and help you answer the question: What can make my sales pitch rise above the rest?

Regardless of whether you're presenting in person, via video conferencing or over the telephone, mastering the following thirteen habits will help you present with confidence.

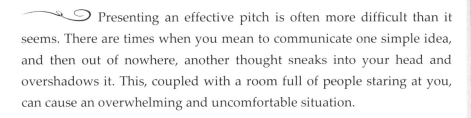

Presenting an effective pitch is often more difficult than it seems. There are times when you mean to communicate one simple idea, and then out of nowhere, another thought sneaks into your head and overshadows it. This, coupled with a room full of people staring at you, can cause an overwhelming and uncomfortable situation.

Even though studies have shown that individuals fear public speaking more than heights, spiders, financial problems and sometimes death itself, those sales representatives who strive to deliver a dynamic message are able to overcome any and all apprehension. In order to transform fear and release all doubt, you must first recognize there is nothing wrong with feeling fearful: It is a universal phenomenon. What is important is how you manage it.

It's guaranteed, giving a presentation will cause a certain amount of stress. The resulting anxiety can manifest itself through physical changes such as sweating, trembling hands, a nervous stomach, accelerated breathing or increased heart rate. If this happens, don't lose your composure. Such symptoms are absolutely normal. The trick is to turn the fear and nervousness into positive energy.

To overcome these challenges, it is important to focus primarily on five basic techniques. They will assist you in maintaining poise while controlling your environment, allowing your confidence to increase.

**Be organized** — Preparation breeds confidence and being organized is where it begins. One of the greatest human fears is that of simply failing. When salespeople are organized, failure is unlikely. More times than not, when your head is clear and you are confident about your message, a positive outcome will occur. Being organized doesn't stop once you have completed all the finishing touches of your pitch; it should continue until you close the sale.

115

**Breathe** — Before ever stepping in front of the prospect, take a number of deep breaths. Slow your body down and feel the air enter and exit your lungs. At the beginning of your pitch and throughout, make a conscious effort to pause and breathe.

**Open your voice** — A few minutes before offering your message, clear your voice softly. While doing this, rotate your jaw in different directions. This will help relax not only your voice, but your facial muscles as well.

**Clear your head** — Concentration is essential to a successful presentation. Prior to the introduction of your message, make a conscious effort to clear your head of any distractions. Focus on your opening remarks and stay calm and relaxed. Fill your brain with positive ideas that equal a successful outcome.

**Stretch** — Prior to stepping in front of the prospect, find a corner where you can stretch. Suggested areas are in the parking garage, restroom or somewhere else out of sight of the potential client. Performing a series of basic stretches will lessen your anxiety that much more. When your body is at ease, the delivery of your pitch will be enhanced.

Polished presenters understand that fear and anxiety can act as stimulants which fuel enthusiasm during a presentation. Through using the above techniques, you can learn to redirect your stress and allow it to give you a more dynamic sales pitch. The bottom line is this: Your insecurities and fear are manageable, but to really release all doubt you must step up to the plate and make your pitch, time and time again. The more often you step in front of the prospect, the more at ease you will become.

> "IT TAKES TWO TO SPEAK TRUTH,
> ONE TO SPEAK AND ANOTHER
> TO HEAR."
> ~ HENRY DAVID THOREAU

# THOROUGH PREPARATION IS KEY

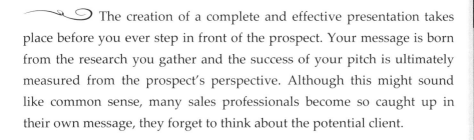 The creation of a complete and effective presentation takes place before you ever step in front of the prospect. Your message is born from the research you gather and the success of your pitch is ultimately measured from the prospect's perspective. Although this might sound like common sense, many sales professionals become so caught up in their own message, they forget to think about the potential client.

If you consider how you react on the receiving end of a sales pitch, you will realize that your presentation's success or failure depends on taking the listener's perspective into account. It is essential to not become bogged down with your material, thereby overshadowing your awareness of the prospect.

Prior to your presentation, enter into a free-flowing dialogue with the potential client by conducting an extensive questioning period. Closely listen and observe the prospect, and work any information gained during this exchange into your message. Properly executed, your questioning period will uncover the primary needs and wants of the prospect. You will have a greater understanding of the potential customer's expectations if questions such as the following are answered:

- What information is the prospect expecting to gather from my pitch?
- How does my product or service meet the potential client's needs or wants?
- Are there any specific guidelines surrounding the format of the presentation?
- Who will be in attendance?
- Will my competitors be pitching, too?

By applying the knowledge learned from the answers to these questions, you will be much more prepared to give a complete and effective presentation. In addition to this type of fact-finding mission, make time to research specific details surrounding the prospect and business. Company history, statistics and significant facts will assist you tremendously as you specifically tailor your message to the potential client.

Make it a habit to always arrive early for your presentations and remember that before you can ask anyone to listen to your pitch, you must believe in it yourself. If you don't have complete trust in your message, the prospect will detect your lack of confidence and knowledge of the subject matter. Without confidence, your presentation will be in great jeopardy. One of the best ways to gain confidence is by thorough preparation.

> UNCERTAINTY PRODUCES
> STRESS THAT HAS A DIRECT
> EFFECT ON THE END RESULT.

# Arrange a Comfortable Structure

The arrangement of a comfortable structure pays hefty dividends when wanting to master the art of offering a successful sales pitch. To present a seamless presentation, your message should consist of the following areas:

## Introduction

The introduction of your presentation serves as the launching pad for your entire pitch. Studies have shown that the average prospect will only listen to the first three minutes of a message before making a conscious decision to either continue listening or tune you out.

Your introduction must be compelling and welcoming. It should identify for the potential client who you are, what you are presenting and why being attentive will be of benefit. Then, in order to grab the prospect's attention, your introduction should be closely followed by an appropriate lead-in to the presentation. In the seven-step sales call, this is known as the opening statement.

## Opening statement

Your opening statement can consist of an attention-getting story about your product or service, a humorous anecdote or an observation that automatically piques the potential customer's interest. Regardless of which method you employ, focus on capturing attention in your opening by:

- Satisfying curiosity
- Showing value and benefits
- Offering your assistance

As soon as you complete your introduction and opening statement, the prospect will be eagerly awaiting your presentation's talking points.

## Talking points

Using clear and decisive talking points is just as important for a sales representative as an architect using blueprints when building a new structure. Your points of interest lead the potential client down the path you have designated. They also provide an explanation of why you believe wholeheartedly in not just your product or service, but in what you have to say.

Talking points are key for keeping yourself on track, in addition to helping the prospect pay close attention and maintain interest in your pitch. The reality is this: Without effective talking points, the odds of becoming nervous and losing confidence in your ability to offer a successful pitch increase greatly.

Once you have introduced your main points of interest, you are ready to continue with the body of your presentation. Depending on the time allotted, you'll spend as much time as necessary delivering your pitch.

## Closing

Think of the best play you have ever seen, the best movie, the greatest concert, the finest novel. How did it end? Powerfully! The potential client's receptiveness is usually highest at the beginning and end of an effective presentation—even if unaware the end is coming.

In order to take full advantage of this effect, it is essential to emphasize and drive home your product or service's main points one last time during your closing. Once you have done this, you are ready to make a memorable argument that will convince the prospect to invest in what you have to offer.

Keep in mind, a powerful closing contains three steps: summarize your product or service and the value and benefits it offers, respectfully ask for a commitment from the prospect, and listen intently to any last-minute questions or concerns. Use positive language and maintain your self-confidence throughout your closing.

If you haven't already mastered the various techniques used in closing a presentation, study them thoroughly and reference them often. Develop your own repertoire of powerful closes that fits your product or service and feels most comfortable. Practice them often to increase the certainty of your success.

> "IT USUALLY TAKES MORE THAN THREE WEEKS TO PREPARE A GOOD IMPROMPTU SPEECH."
> ~ MARK TWAIN

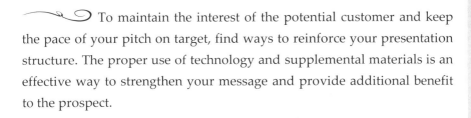

# UTILIZE SUPPORTING MATERIALS

To maintain the interest of the potential customer and keep the pace of your pitch on target, find ways to reinforce your presentation structure. The proper use of technology and supplemental materials is an effective way to strengthen your message and provide additional benefit to the prospect.

Once your presentation has been constructed, the decision needs to be made about what type of visual aids you plan to use. Resources such as blow-ups, computer-projected slides, flip charts and various handouts are all mediums readily available to be worked into your pitch. The use of photographs, charts and graphics adds value to the content as well. Utilizing these types of tools gives your message variety, while keeping it interesting.

Bear in mind, though, the primary reason for using visual aids is to emphasize the major points of your presentation. Don't rely on them to become the main highlight of your message. The substance of your pitch is you and what you have to offer; therefore, you must be the primary medium for delivering the information on your product or service. Avoid hiding behind the visual aids or speaking to them. If you do, you are likely to lose rapport with the prospect and the impact of your pitch will suffer. Make your presentation people-centered, not media-centered.

Whether using a flip chart, slideshow or any other medium, maintain an easy-to-read layout. Use visual aids to display images and key words or phrases that summarize and support your main points. This approach will be much more effective and will not overwhelm the prospect during the entire presentation process.

It is important to also determine what "leave-behind" items you will employ. These can serve as a call to action or function as a great referral source after your pitch is complete. They are also useful in supplying necessary supporting data without cluttering your visual aids. Simplicity is essential. Leave behind only what is crucial and can be easily reviewed.

> TO CHANGE OTHERS' BEHAVIOR, YOU MUST BEGIN BY CHANGING THEIR PERSPECTIVE.

# BECOME FAMILIAR WITH YOUR SURROUNDINGS

Be aware of the environment surrounding the potential client when presenting a pitch. Is the room comfortable and conducive to an effective presentation? Everything from room temperature to lighting to the position of the podium and chairs is relevant to your approach.

When using props and multi-media equipment, make sure each person will be able to clearly see your visuals. If you feel the quality of your presentation will be enhanced by a simple adjustment, ask to make a change. Be respectful of the prospect's time, never encroaching on a potential client's hospitality.

How you approach the specifics of the venue where you will be making your pitch is incredibly significant. Never underestimate the importance of every detail while minimizing outside distractions. Realize that it's the little things that often make the greatest impressions.

> **WHEN INDIVIDUALS ARE AT EASE, THEY ARE MORE LIKELY TO ABSORB YOUR MESSAGE.**

THIRTEEN HABITS OF PITCHING WITH CONFIDENCE

# Develop a Dynamic Delivery

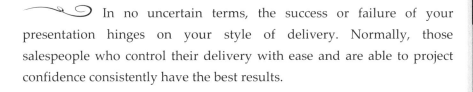

In no uncertain terms, the success or failure of your presentation hinges on your style of delivery. Normally, those salespeople who control their delivery with ease and are able to project confidence consistently have the best results.

When wanting to develop a dynamic delivery, a good place to begin is by recognizing your own unique style. Are you comfortable with using humor throughout your message, or is your energetic personality what you would like the prospect to focus on? Are you more at ease behind a podium or out in front? These are the types of questions that are worth answering when wanting to define what works best for the strengths of your presentation style.

Research shows that 55% of your pitch's impact is determined by your posture, gestures and eye contact; 30% by your voice tone and inflection; and only 15% by the content of your presentation. Along these lines, it is important to keep in mind that there are other factors that affect the success of your delivery as well. The following is an in-depth list for your reference.

**Body language:** This factor has a tremendous impact on the potential customer. Whether addressing one person or ten, people are continually responding, both consciously and subconsciously, to what your body language is saying.

**Posture:** One of the most fundamental statements you make with your body is your posture. Regardless of whether you are seated or standing, an aligned, upright position communicates a message of confidence and integrity. It says that you are together and on top of your game. People are watching you from the minute you enter the room to the moment you leave. How you carry yourself sets an important tone.

**Voluntary movements:** Movements you make while presenting your message have a great influence on the prospect. Unnecessary, subconscious actions such as swaying, rocking or pacing will distract and possibly annoy the potential client. Turning your back toward the prospect will attract negative attention, too. Awareness is the secret to freeing yourself from these types of movements and is best acquired when videotaping or watching yourself in a mirror. As your awareness increases through practice, you will find it easier to move in a manner that is natural and uninhibited.

**Eye contact:** Making eye contact is a humanizing element in an often impersonal world. It is a crucial aspect of communication and thus an important part of every successful presentation. Eye contact should be a simple, natural expression of your interest in the potential client, allowing you to monitor the prospect's awareness and understanding of what you are offering.

If presenting to more than a single individual, be certain to look at the various people in the room, not just the person in charge. You don't want to direct your remarks to one person, nor do you want to seem to ignore everyone else. At times this can be difficult, but this one variable is significant. Sales representatives who don't look prospects in the eye run the risk of coming across as insincere. Good visual contact automatically illustrates the confidence you have in yourself and in your product or service. It opens the channel of communication and establishes rapport, involving the potential customer in the presentation and personalizing the message.

**Personal appearance:** Your appearance carries substantial value while you have the attention of a potential client. Develop the habit of dressing properly for the occasion. It's best not to overdress or underdress, depending on the prospect you are speaking to. Professionalism is the key, and your appearance is a direct link to how you are perceived before, during and after the presentation. In general, avoid excess. Keep patterns, accessories and colors simple. You should be the focus—not what you're wearing.

**Energy and enthusiasm:** The personality you project during your pitch will separate you from many other sales professionals and can become your point of difference. Allow the excitement from your voice as well as your body language to captivate the potential client. Most individuals would rather listen to a sales representative who brings a smile to their face than one who doesn't. An easy way of doing this is through the excitement projected in your body movements and gestures. Keep in mind, you always want to work toward a balanced approach—not overly excited, but not flat either. Also, stay within a reasonable distance from the prospect, making sure not to encroach upon the potential client's personal space.

**Voice variance:** A major impact on the delivery of your message, your voice alone has many shades of meaning that can be communicated with great expression. It should be natural, decisive and clear. You can refine your voice by recognizing and eliminating unnecessary elements in your vocal usage. In order to do this, you must first learn how to pause, realize the importance of pacing and control your volume.

*Pausing* is a natural part of speaking, yet anxiety often causes salespeople to fill their pauses with "uhmms, uhhhs, you knows" and other unnecessary, distracting noises. Learning to pause appropriately is the single most important element in making the most of your voice, and one of the most effective tools to use when making a point. It gives you the opportunity to think about what to say next and to hear what you just said. A pause allows you time to collect yourself and breathe fully, giving the prospect time to assimilate your message and feel more relaxed.

Many sales representatives talk too fast, often speeding up as their presentation progresses. They forget to *pace* themselves. This can cause poor articulation, slurring or swallowing of words, and a loss of contact with the potential customer. Speed-talking usually occurs because of nervousness or overexcitement. Never allow yourself to be hurried as you speak, even if you are running short on time. Set a comfortable pace for comprehension.

In order to make full use of your expressive abilities, be certain that the prospect can hear what you are saying. If you're not sure you can be heard or if you think you are too loud, ask the prospect for feedback and modulate your *volume* accordingly. Raising and lowering your voice appropriately are essential to effective speaking. Your voice is a naturally expressive instrument. The movement of tone and inflection gives your voice life. It allows you greater scope for emphasizing your message points.

**Breathing:** When nervousness and anxiety arrive, many sales professionals forget to breathe. As important as voice fluctuation, breathing frequently not only fuels your voice, it will relax you and help you speak clearly and decisively. Before ever beginning a sales pitch, make it a habit to find a quiet place and take a number of deep, steady breaths. This will assist you greatly as you focus on the task at hand.

**Assessing the response:** Gauging the prospect's response during your presentation is a critical element of a dynamic delivery. Learn to read the potential client while offering your message so proper adjustments can be made if needed. The continuous response, either verbal or nonverbal, will dictate the direction you travel during your pitch. For example, if the prospect seems bored and uninterested in a segment of your presentation, you must be able to read this communication and make adjustments. Over time, you will become constantly aware of the response you are receiving. Once you have mastered this skill, you'll be able to make the necessary adjustments during your pitch while presenting with total confidence.

**Building mutual respect:** Mutual respect should be a major goal of every salesperson. As an ambassador for your product or service, you want to convey its potential as well as your own knowledge and belief. You would like the prospect to respect your abilities and professional judgment in addition to what you are offering for purchase. To be successful at this, you must be the one to extend respect first. For example, when giving your pitch to a group, speak to each person individually prior to beginning, starting with your primary contact. Take time to introduce yourself and ask questions about each one's business and interests. Show that you not only respect them as business professionals, but more importantly as human beings. From the words you choose to speak to the images and supporting materials you decide to share, respect for every individual observing your presentation needs to be a priority.

> "TO BE A WINNER YOU MUST PLAN TO WIN, PREPARE TO WIN AND EXPECT TO WIN."
> ~ ZIG ZIGLAR

# Encourage Questions & Answers

Encouraging the potential client to ask questions gives the opportunity to reinforce the communication you have established during your presentation and allows you to check the prospect's comprehension in the event you are delivering technical information or complicated ideas.

If speaking to a group, actively seek questions by stepping toward your audience, raising a hand slightly and stating, "I will be happy to answer any questions." This practice will encourage an orderly question and answer session.

Pause and wait, and then listen attentively as each question is being asked. Look directly at the person posing the question. This demonstrates respect and forces you to focus on the question at hand. After listening to the question, take time to breathe and pause. Compliment the question, if possible. A simple "Good question" is often enough. If all audience participants are unable to hear the question, make sure to repeat it out loud before providing a response. Give honest, simple and straight-forward answers. When offering your response, direct it to the entire group. While one person asks the question, the whole group waits for the response.

Be prepared for people who may be discouraging or combative. If faced with a hostile question or comment, remember these three easy steps:

- Acknowledge feelings, facts or both.
- Give an informative response.
- Maintain your position with composure.

It is always helpful during the preparation of a message to anticipate what questions may be asked and prepare your answers in advance.

Remember, maintain the same style and demeanor while answering questions that you used during your presentation.

> "IT WASN'T SO MUCH THAT I WAS ALL ALONE ON STAGE, BUT THE REALIZATION OF HOW MUCH I NEEDED A RESPONSE."
> ~ LORETTA SWIT

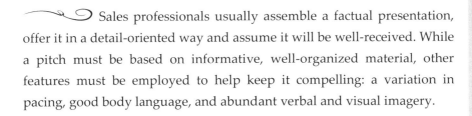

Sales professionals usually assemble a factual presentation, offer it in a detail-oriented way and assume it will be well-received. While a pitch must be based on informative, well-organized material, other features must be employed to help keep it compelling: a variation in pacing, good body language, and abundant verbal and visual imagery.

Why is this? Researchers have found that an individual's brain tends to focus on the body language, rhythm and imagery that presenters deliver more than the words spoken. These "right hemisphere" elements are more engaging than the words themselves.

To ensure your presentation is engaging and successful, you must use your whole brain, integrating imagery and intuition with logic and analysis. Only by using both sides of your brain—the logical and the imaginative—will you be able to communicate fully with the brain of the potential client.

It is always smart to be on the lookout for anything that can help improve your skills. For instance, the following are a few suggestions:

- Every chance you have to practice is one more opportunity to improve your message. Rehearsing prior to a live sales pitch will help calm your nerves and build confidence. It will also help you with the timing and transition of each area of your presentation structure. If possible, videotape and study your rehearsal or have a group of close friends observe your practice session and offer you feedback.

- Watch other salespeople whenever possible to learn new ideas, techniques and styles. You will be surprised how quickly you learn what is effective and what isn't.

- Join a local Toastmasters club or other civic group. This will help you become more involved, give you access to good resources and provide you with frequent opportunities to present a variety of messages.

- When appropriate, hand out evaluation forms, ask questions of prospects and invite feedback from colleagues. It is extremely helpful to ask for constructive criticism as often as possible. This is how to ensure that every facet of your pitch will improve.

- Create a journal to help plan and evaluate each of your presentations. Use this resource to record information about the potential client, your objectives, the specifics of your pitch and your successful experiences. After each presentation, objectively measure your strengths and weaknesses and record them.

- Take a few minutes each day to expand your vocabulary. Pull out your dictionary and randomly select five words. Practice pronouncing the word, memorize the spelling and, after reading the definition, mentally construct a sentence using each word. You can also benefit by looking for unfamiliar words while keeping up with current events.

- Invest in a professional presentation coach who will assess your current level of expertise, while constructing a plan for future improvement. Employing a specialist who will not only work with you one-on-one, but who will also video your pitches and critique them is a smart expenditure.

As you continue sharpening your skills as a sales representative, place yourself and your product or service in a positive light and be willing to refine your presentation style. You'll be glad you did!

> **"SPEECH IS POWER: SPEECH IS TO PERSUADE, TO CONVERT, TO COMPEL."**
> ~ RALPH WALDO EMERSON

# TECHNIQUES OF A SALES PROFESSIONAL

It is important to remember that the slides used during your presentation are not the messenger; they are simply your communication aids. Below are ten rules to follow when preparing slides:

- Present no more than three to five key points per slide.
- Make text and numbers legible.
- Use color carefully.
- Make visuals large enough to view clearly.
- Graph data.
- Make pictures and diagrams easy to see.
- Avoid unnecessary slides.
- When using animations, spread them equally throughout.
- Use slides sparingly.
- Make slides pictorial.

In addition, there are a few simple communication techniques to always adhere to:

- Be articulate and know your presentation.
- Be curious and engaged with the prospect.
- Be both patient and assertive.
- Know when to ask questions.
- Know when to speak and listen.

> "OUR POWER TO COMMUNICATE DETERMINES THE LEVEL OF OUR INFLUENCE."
> ~ RUDOLPH GIULIANI

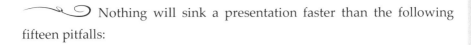
Nothing will sink a presentation faster than the following fifteen pitfalls:

- The lack of sound preparation
- Reading your message verbatim to the prospect
- Bragging about yourself too frequently during the pitch
- Telling an inappropriate joke that offends the prospect
- Making little eye contact with the potential client
- Presenting poor visual aids that are hard to read
- Using distracting motions that the prospect picks up on
- Not knowing the potential customer
- Lacking volume control in your voice
- Failing to add excitement and energy into your message
- Not arriving at the presentation venue on time
- Forgetting to provide time for questions and answers
- Dressing inappropriately
- Not pacing the speed of your voice while presenting your pitch
- Simply not having fun while giving your presentation

> "IF YOU TAKE RESPONSIBILITY
> FOR YOURSELF YOU WILL
> DEVELOP A HUNGER TO
> ACCOMPLISH YOUR DREAMS."
> ~ LES BROWN

# Checklist for Your Presentation

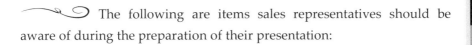 The following are items sales representatives should be aware of during the preparation of their presentation:

**Computer hardware and software:** Always check your equipment immediately before the pitch to make sure all systems are functioning. Have extra cords and batteries available as well as a backup plan in the event of a malfunction.

**Flip chart:** Is there enough paper? Do you have a supply of marking pens? Have you checked to make sure the pens have not dried out?

**Leave-behinds:** Are collateral materials easily accessible and in order so they can be distributed with minimum disruption?

**Lighting:** Try to leave on as many lights as possible. Be aware of glare on the projection screen as well as clarity of the slides if natural lighting is prevalent.

**Seating arrangement:** If you have control over seating in the room, exercise it. If possible, arrange the seating so that the prospect or prospects have an unimpeded view of your visual aids.

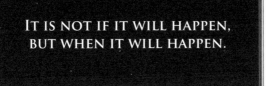

IT IS NOT IF IT WILL HAPPEN,
BUT WHEN IT WILL HAPPEN.

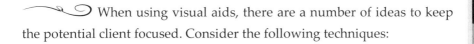
When using visual aids, there are a number of ideas to keep the potential client focused. Consider the following techniques:

- Do not speak until you have made eye contact with the prospect. If using visuals, look at the screen momentarily to recall the point you want to make and then turn to the potential customer and deliver it.

- When appropriate, temporarily black out the screen to focus the prospect's attention from the LCD projected slide to you. If using an overhead, shut it off when giving a lengthy explanation; however, don't turn it on and off frequently.

- Turn a flip chart page when you have finished referring to it. If preparing a flip chart in advance, leave one or two blank pages between each prepared sheet to obscure the next page.

- Erase the whiteboard when you are finished making a point.

- Demonstrate an object at the appropriate time and then cover it up when no longer needed. Walk over to the prospect, show it briefly and make it available at the end of the presentation for viewing.

> "WITH EVERY EXPERIENCE, YOU ALONE ARE PAINTING YOUR OWN CANVAS, THOUGHT BY THOUGHT, CHOICE BY CHOICE."
> ~ OPRAH WINFREY

143

# Assess Your Presentation Skills

The following are fifteen questions to ask yourself when preparing for a presentation:

- Have I thoroughly researched and analyzed the prospect?
- Have I determined basic objectives for my pitch?
- Have I built my message around my talking points?
- Have I incorporated a preview and a review of my main ideas?
- Have I developed an attention-getting introduction?
- Does my closing include a call to action?
- Are my visual tools carefully prepared and understandable?
- Do the visual aids I plan to use enhance my pitch or hinder it?
- Do I plan to use energy and enthusiasm in my presentation?
- Have I rehearsed while standing and using my visual tools?
- Have I prepared answers to anticipated questions?
- Have I checked my electronic equipment prior to my pitch?
- Do I plan to maintain good eye contact at all times?
- Do I plan to use movements and gestures that are natural?
- Do I plan to use a strong and clear voice with good inflection?

> "ENTHUSIASM IS THE GREATEST ASSET IN THE WORLD. IT BEATS MONEY, POWER AND INFLUENCE."
> ~ HENRY CHESTER

# TWENTY TIPS TO PROVIDING QUALITY CUSTOMER CARE

# INTRODUCTION

Given the complexity of today's global economy, businesses now more than ever are challenged with distinguishing themselves from their competition. Providing quality customer care consistently to those who choose to invest in your product or service is a beneficial way to do just that.

Sam Walton, founder of Wal-Mart, once said, "There is only one boss and whether a person shines shoes for a living or heads up the biggest corporation in the world, the boss remains the same. It is the customer! The customer is the person who pays everyone's salary and who decides whether a business is going to succeed or fail. In fact, the customer can fire everybody in the company from the chairman on down, and he can do it simply by spending his money elsewhere. Literally everything we do, every concept perceived, every technology developed and associate employed, is directed with this one objective in mind—pleasing the customer." Regardless of the industry, all businesses rely on loyal patrons. Without them a business will fail.

The tips presented in this second bonus section serve as a reminder of the many basic fundamentals of providing quality customer care and the impact each has on your overall success as a sales representative. As you work toward increasing your client base, not only meeting but exceeding the customer's expectations, the following practices should be a quick source to refer to often.

Remember, a typical business hears from only 4% of its dissatisfied customers. The other 96% just quietly go away and 91% will never come back. That represents a serious financial loss for salespeople who do not know how to treat clients and a tremendous gain for those who do. Providing quality customer care in any business begins with treating people with respect, sharing the right attitude, providing a clean atmosphere and never forgetting to listen to the client first. The following twenty tips will help you rise above the competition.

149

# RECOGNIZE THE FUNDAMENTALS OF YOUR CUSTOMER

⎯⎯⌒⌒ Understanding the fundamentals of your customer is a critical component of your quality customer care approach. This type of knowledge contributes to the success of any salesperson—in any business.

Providing quality customer care is not just about the exchange of monies for a product or service, it is about true satisfaction as well. Research shows if a patron walks away not just content, but actually satisfied with the purchase, the customer will return time and time again.

When analyzing the essentials of your clients, consider dividing them into three basic categories:

- Customers who know exactly what they want
- Customers who are not sure what they want, but have a need
- Customers who do not know if they want or need anything

Those sales professionals who make it a priority to understand the meaning behind providing quality customer care know that customers bring us their needs and wants. It's our privilege to serve them. Their opinions of us and our work are our most valuable assets.

Customers expect value for their money. If they don't receive value, they'll go elsewhere. Every client who walks through the door expects to be acknowledged, no matter what the situation. As Henry Ford, the founder of Ford Motor Company, once said, "Customers are the bosses behind our bosses. Without them, we won't get paid."

No matter how busy you ever become, remember: Customers are the most important people ever in the office...in person, by telephone, by mail or e-mail. Customers are not dependent on you...you are dependent on them. They are not an interruption of your work...they are the purpose of it.

A customer is not someone to argue or match wits with; no one has ever won an argument with a customer. By understanding the fundamentals of a customer and putting that knowledge to work for you, your reputation for excellent care will create a long-term relationship with your clients, bringing satisfaction not only to them but to you as well.

> "OUR GREATEST ASSET IS THE CUSTOMER! TREAT EACH CUSTOMER AS IF THEY ARE THE ONLY ONE!"
> ~ LAURICE LEITAO

# Define Quality Customer Care

Suppose your team leader has asked you to pick up an important package from a local insurance agency. Once you arrive at the office, a receptionist at the front desk greets you. As you are making your request for the package, the receptionist's cellular telephone begins to ring. Without saying a word to you, she turns in the opposite direction, answers the telephone and proceeds to carry on a five-minute conversation.

Most likely you have found yourself in this type of scenario at one time or another. How did it make you feel? Knowing that situations like this occur more often than not, those who want to improve upon their customer service skills should ask themselves a few important questions:

- What does the term "customer" mean to me?
- Who are my customers and what do they expect?
- What is my definition of quality customer care?
- Why is it important that I exceed my customer's expectations?
- What are some ways I inadvertently disrespect my customers?

The standard definition of customer care is providing a quality product or service that satisfies the needs and wants of a customer and keeps that client coming back. As simple as this might seem, there are also a few other important elements that make up the true meaning of quality customer care.

Many people are familiar with computer giant Dell's customer-focused direct business model. Less well known is the unique environment forged by founder Michael Dell since the company was founded in 1984. That environment is characterized in a statement of corporate philosophy called the "Soul of Dell." It defines the kind of company Dell is and aspires to become, serves as a guide for its actions around the world and, ultimately, forms the basis of its "winning culture."

153

As a successful sales representative, you must define your own customer care and sales philosophy and stand behind it. "Where should I begin?" you might ask. Begin by looking inward.

Recall an establishment you enjoy doing business with. Aside from the product or service provided, why do you spend your hard-earned money there? Is it because the company exemplifies effective qualities such as timeliness, friendliness, flexibility, common courtesy and so forth? It not only satisfies your needs and wants, but more importantly exceeds your expectations. You truly come to rely on its level of care and anything less is not acceptable.

On the other hand, call to mind a business you've stopped patronizing in the past. What qualities contributed to your lack of satisfaction? Unfriendly people, gruff service, the lack of empathy, inefficient processing—do any of these ring a bell? In the end, you feel mistreated, unsatisfied and taken advantage of.

Consumer satisfaction, repeat business, increased profits, positive morale, strong teamwork and expansion are all tied into the definition of quality customer care. Define your philosophy and put it into practice and you will achieve long-lasting, positive results.

> "WE NEED TO GIVE OUR CUSTOMERS SOMETHING MORE, AND THAT SOMETHING MORE MAY JUST BE LOVE."
> ~ CHEESECAKE FACTORY

# RECOGNIZE THE VOICE OF YOUR CUSTOMER

Samantha Woods enters the upscale clothing store where you have been employed for over a year. She is a very good patron, one you have assisted on prior occasions. Ordinarily, you would walk over and offer your help; however, you are currently assisting another client. None of your colleagues acknowledge that Ms. Woods has entered the boutique or offer their assistance. Fifteen minutes pass and the circumstances are still the same. With obvious displeasure, she turns around and leaves. How will she remember her visit and, better yet, who will she tell?

A customer's voice is the voice of a business. Key consumer sector data has revealed the following:

- Customers will spend up to 10% more for the same product with better service.
- When customers receive good service, each one tells 10 to 12 people on average; a dissatisfied customer will tell upwards of 20 people about the experience.
- If a complaint is resolved in their favor, 7 out of 10 customers will continue doing business with you.
- There is an 82% chance customers will repurchase from a company where they were satisfied.
- The average business spends 6 times more to attract new customers than it does to keep old ones.
- There is a 91% chance that poor service will dissuade a customer from ever returning to a company.

These statistics, coupled with the fact that word of mouth is incredibly potent, should be reason enough for all salespeople to take note of the power of the patron's voice.

What prompts a customer to tell others about a personal experience, good or bad? What effect does the patron have on potential clients? Take a step back once again and consider your own encounters as a paying customer.

If you received outstanding care, did you share your experience with anyone? Perhaps you encouraged someone to purchase a product or service based on your own satisfaction.

Then again, an experience may have been less than ideal. If you were dissatisfied, did you share your frustration with others? How long did you harbor negative feelings? Did you lodge a complaint or voice your displeasure? The U.S. Office of Consumer Affairs reports that only 4% of dissatisfied customers complain to the company. The reality is the vast, silent majority would rather switch than fight.

It is important to remember that customers have long memories. They cherish individuals who treat them well and quickly stop patronizing those who don't.

> "HERE IS A SIMPLE BUT POWERFUL RULE: ALWAYS GIVE PEOPLE MORE THAN WHAT THEY EXPECT TO GET."
> ~ NELSON BOSWELL

# MASTER THE ART OF READING BODY LANGUAGE

∽◯ Have you ever been around a sales professional who seemed to understand what a customer's needs and wants were before any verbal communication ever took place? Odds are that individual has mastered the art of reading body language.

The knack of understanding an individual's body language is a skill that can only be practiced if you are paying close attention. Nonverbal communication can say much more than verbalization at times. Since body language sets the tone for a verbal exchange, make it a point to recognize what is being said before it is ever spoken.

Be conscious of your customer's facial reactions, body posture, hand gestures, attentiveness and the personal space established. When verbal communication is set into motion, pay close attention to the tone of voice that is being used to deliver the message.

Improving your ability to read others' body language is not difficult if you know what signals to look for. To help sharpen your skills, in the table below match each description on the left with a corresponding mood or emotion on the right. Some signals have multiple meanings.

| SIGNAL | MEANS |
|---|---|
| Crossed arms | Smart |
| Avoiding eye contact | Confident |
| Drumming fingers | Enthusiastic |
| Good posture | Sad |
| Leaning back in chair | Angry |
| Head up | Disappointed |
| Hands in pockets | Discouraged |
| Slouching | Upset |
| Eyes cast downward | Insecure |
| Behind a podium or computer monitor | Interested |
| Direct eye contact | Optimistic |
| Palms up | Uninterested |
| Standing still | Tired |
| Hands clasped | Dishonest |
| Lean forward when seated | Unmotivated |

The art of reading your customers' body language will make you more efficient, polite, timely and flexible with your client care and, at the end of a long day, your patrons will truly appreciate the initiative you took to better understand them.

> "EVERYONE IS TRYING TO ACCOMPLISH SOMETHING BIG, NOT REALIZING THAT LIFE IS MADE UP OF LITTLE THINGS."
> ~ FRANK A. CLARK

# Work toward Increasing Customer Retention

Poor customer care generally results in consumer dissatisfaction, lack of returning clients and businesses shutting their doors. Various surveys show that poor customer service is the leading complaint, even ahead of prices, cited by patrons who stop purchasing a company's product or service.

How patrons feel about the people who serve them is a key factor in increasing customer retention and loyalty. After years of polling and market research, it turns out clients are constantly internalizing their customer care experience. What this means is they are measuring a business on the level of customer service received during each transaction—and in the end, the business normally never hears about the marks earned.

While every consumer is different, the following are five basic qualities most businesses and sales representatives are constantly graded on:

**Friendliness:** Clients want to feel as though they are being handled with common courtesy and politeness.

**Empathy:** Customers need to know that the salesperson understands their requests and circumstances.

**Fairness:** Clients want to feel as though they have received adequate attention and reasonable answers.

**Control:** Customers want to feel as though their input has influenced the outcome.

**Information:** Clients want accurate information about the product or service in an efficient and timely manner.

If you are interested in examining your effectiveness when dealing with consumers, reflect closely on the following questions:

- Do you project an honest, straightforward image?
- Do you think your clients receive excellent service from you that they might not receive elsewhere?
- From the buyer's point of view, would you be described as reliable?
- Do you think your customers find you to be knowledgeable about your product or service and an accurate source of industry information?
- Whenever possible, do you handle clients' complaints to their satisfaction?
- Do your customers believe that you have their personal well-being at heart?
- Do you place a high value on personal integrity?
- Would most of your clients still deal with you, even if the competitor had lower prices?

Take time to scrutinize your answers and use the information to improve your level of client care. The results can have a great impact on your level of customer retention.

> **AS FAR AS CUSTOMERS ARE CONCERNED YOU ARE THE COMPANY. YOU HOLD IN YOUR HANDS THE POWER TO KEEP CUSTOMERS COMING BACK.**

As previously covered, customers determine how profitable a business is. Treated well, they will be your greatest source of advertising and promotion. Provided with good value, they will continue to reward you with their dollars and cents for years to come.

One way to ensure quality customer care is by extending a positive attitude to each patron you come into contact with. Not just every once in a while, but all the time.

Individuals choose daily what attitude to possess. Their outlook can be either positive or negative. In both cases, their mind-set is extremely contagious.

---

## THE IMPORTANCE OF ATTITUDE

- Listen to your customers first
- Show off your smile
- Don't tell clients your problems
- Acknowledge your customers' feelings
- Make good eye contact
- Don't overpromise
- Send thank you notes when feasible
- Compliment your clients when appropriate
- Don't take your customers' anger personally
- Apologize for any problems
- Say thank you
- Have a good tone of voice

---

The disposition projected to "external" clients should be no different than the one projected to fellow employees. Most sales representatives who go the extra mile for their patrons will also do the same for their co-workers.

Put it this way, have you ever caught someone else's yawn? Just like yawns, attitudes are easy to catch, and negative attitudes have a major ripple effect. When you help your clients and colleagues catch your positive, helpful and cheerful mood, you're making yourself infinitely more valuable. In turn, you are exemplifying quality customer care, which not only will affect your company's bottom line, but yours as well.

> "ONE OF THE DEEP SECRETS OF LIFE IS THAT ALL THAT IS REALLY WORTH DOING IS WHAT WE DO FOR OTHERS."
> ~ LEWIS CARROLL

# Make a Memorable First Impression

As you have read, there are many components to providing quality customer care. However, regardless of the level of your service, the first impression you make on your patrons will influence their opinion of you throughout all of their dealings, perhaps even dictating whether they will frequent your establishment or not.

You will only get one chance to make a memorable first impression. In a matter of seconds, the customer will make a judgment based on simple observations. You can increase your odds by making a concerted effort to embrace the following practices:

- Maintain a pleasant look on your face and smile naturally.
- Avoid chewing gum, tobacco or smoking in front of clients.
- Look professional in dress and appearance.
- Greet customers within one minute of their arrival.
- Ask how you can assist the patron.
- Make eye contact with all clients.
- Speak with a pleasant tone of voice.
- Always use courteous words like "thank you" and "please."
- Give clients comprehensive information about your business.
- Be the first to apologize for mistakes or inconveniences.
- Be a friendly, helpful and sincere person.
- Be able to give good directions to other places of interest.

Warm, friendly people immediately gain favor with others. What they say is often openly accepted, trusted and believed. Making a memorable first impression will create a pleasant, lasting relationship with your customer.

> **A SALE IS NOT SOMETHING YOU PURSUE; IT IS SOMETHING THAT HAPPENS WHILE YOU ARE IMMERSED IN SERVING YOUR CUSTOMER.**

163

# Never Underestimate Appearance

Regardless of how you choose to dress, your appearance has a huge effect on the image you project. It's a well-known fact: People draw conclusions very quickly. In the blink of an eye, you have the ability to influence others' thoughts and opinions of both you and your business through your overall appearance.

For example, what better way to sell clothing or cosmetics in a large department store than to see well-groomed, nicely dressed salespeople serving clients? This has become a global industry standard simply because it works. People like to buy products from sales representatives who look good in the very products they are offering. Customers imagine themselves looking like the fashionable salesperson.

It's important to remember that you may be your customers' only impression of the business you represent. The way you are perceived could be winning or losing them. Do not be mistaken; appearance is only one piece of the puzzle, but it is a very important piece—the most successful salespeople are also well trained and informed about their products, services and companies.

> **BE EVERYWHERE, DO EVERYTHING AND NEVER FAIL TO ASTONISH THE CUSTOMER.**

# Relate Through Your Own Experience

Providing quality customer care means understanding the needs, wants, concerns and emotions of your client. When making a concentrated effort to do this, you automatically increase the odds of exceeding the overall expectations of each patron who walks through your door.

To employ such a concept, draw on your own experiences as a customer. What goes through your mind before investing in a product or service? What captures your interest or turns you off? Does the level of rapport with a particular salesperson really make a difference?

Clients' needs are very important to them; therefore, those needs should be important to you as well. Patrons are more likely to begin allowing relationships to form when they recognize the effort you are making to identify with them. When a connection is made, a bond is created, and the result equals confidence and trust.

> ## CUSTOMER SERVICE IS AN ACUTE AWARENESS OF NEEDS, PROBLEMS, FEARS AND ASPIRATIONS.

# It's the Little Things

At any given time, an existing or potential customer may approach you for tidbits of helpful information. Directions, points of interest, bank locations, church information, family activities, recreational facilities, child-friendly restaurants and entertainment are just a few items of possible interest.

Being informed, not only about the specifics of your product or service but also about your surrounding community, increases your advantage of providing quality customer care.

Consider this short list of questions worth learning the answers to:

- How did this town get its name?
- What is the population?
- Where is the chamber of commerce located?
- Are there any state parks in this area?
- Which three restaurants would you recommend?
- What are the most enjoyable activities for children?
- Where is the closest golf course located?
- Are there any local antique or specialty shops?
- What are the top five things to do and see within the community?

You never know who is about to walk through the door or pick up the telephone to call. Providing useful and accurate information in a time of need speaks volumes for both you and the service you are willing to provide.

> **"EVERY GREAT BUSINESS IS BUILT ON FRIENDSHIP."**
> ~ J.C. PENNEY

# Always Be Kid-Friendly

Your customers are due to arrive any minute to begin looking at new vehicles. The selection process will be lengthy and require minimal distractions and a quiet atmosphere. When they arrive, two of their children are in tow—five and seven years of age. Knowing that you need to devote all of your attention to the clients, what can you do to ensure that their children are safely entertained in order for you to develop and close the sale? How can you better prepare for similar scenarios in the future?

Children are customers just like their parents. Providing a friendly environment that is safe and entertaining keeps kids happy and, in turn, keeps their parents happy, too.

A good rule of thumb is to always remember that parents will respond to you in the same manner in which you respond to their children; friendliness breeds friendliness—irritation breeds irritation. The parents' ability to remain focused and comfortable hinges on knowing that their children are accepted and treated with the same kindness you afford them.

Now granted, there are always instances when parents may do little to control their children, without regard to safety or other customers' feelings. During these times, you may be faced with difficult choices. If you are creative and friendly with unruly children, you can divert potential problems and turn a negative experience into a positive one.

Be prepared to entertain children with puzzles, videos, games or crayons, and also have some light snacks on hand. In today's age of information, there are many free Internet resources for creating games and puzzles of all types and skill levels.

If you subscribe to the theory of doing your best to be kid-friendly today, the children you have extended kindness to may one day become loyal adult customers.

> "FORGET ABOUT THE SALES
> YOU WANT TO MAKE AND
> CONCENTRATE ON THE SERVICE
> YOU WANT TO RENDER."
> ~ HARRY BULLIS

# BE FORTHRIGHT ABOUT RULES AND REGULATIONS

If the customer is initially made aware of the rules and regulations pertaining to your business, product or service, then there should be no misunderstandings, surprises or opportunities for a disappointing outcome.

It is essential to not only be prepared to convey rules and regulations, but also to offer an explanation of why they exist and how the client ultimately benefits from such guidelines. Knowing this, you must fully be aware and understand all company policies and enforce them when needed. At times, you may not agree with the rules and regulations set forth; however, the fact remains they are there for a reason and it is your responsibility to see them through in a positive manner.

As in all things, policies and procedures are subject to change. When this occurs, staying informed lessens potential confusion for repeat customers. If you don't completely understand the purpose and reason behind a guideline, ask for clarification. This will be of tremendous help when having to impose an unpopular rule or regulation. When such a situation occurs, what follows are a few ideas to keep in mind:

- **First, deal with the customer's feeling of inconvenience.** If the client was inconvenienced, apologize on behalf of yourself and your organization.

- **Second, explain why the company follows the policies and procedures.** If you don't know why—find out! Always make it your business to be informed about the key issues that affect your customers.

- **Third, offer an alternative solution.** Propose a variety of suggestions that might be pleasing to your client. While your suggestions may not be taken, at least you have made an attempt and the customer will appreciate that.

Honest communication is pertinent when wanting to provide quality customer care. There is nothing clients appreciate more than your being forthright about rules and regulations on the front end so they can enjoy your product or service on the back end.

> "IF YOU DON'T HAVE TIME TO DO SOMETHING RIGHT, WHEN WILL YOU HAVE TIME TO DO IT OVER?"
>
> ~ JOHN WOODEN

# PROVIDE EFFECTIVE SAFETY MEASURES

Customers want to feel as safe and protected in your place of business as they do in their own homes. You must be aware of problems in and around your establishment that might threaten the physical security of your patrons, such as burned-out lights in parking lots, hazardous spills and suspicious characters. As a standard practice, take immediate steps to rectify any situation you feel may cause harm to a client or another employee.

Not only is a business expected to provide a safe atmosphere, it also has a responsibility to protect the client's identity and financial well-being to the best of its ability. Credit card fraud and identity theft are two of the most common types of theft today. It can take years to rebuild a financial profile and resolve lingering problems after unscrupulous thieves strike. Most customers will not become irritated if you question their identity thoroughly. They understand that by doing so you are protecting them both personally and financially. Sales representatives should always be alert and diligent when engaging in a financial transaction, with knowledge and understanding of the proper steps to take if they suspect fraud.

By providing all-around, effective safety measures, your patrons will not only feel safe, they will be safe.

> DON'T EVER UNDERESTIMATE
> THE IMPORTANCE OF SAFETY.
> CIRCUMSTANCES CAN CHANGE
> IN THE BLINK OF AN EYE.

TWENTY TIPS TO PROVIDING QUALITY CUSTOMER CARE

# Become Familiar With the Unfamiliar

No one likes to experience unpredictable circumstances where there is danger to life, limb or property. However, the fact remains that accidents do happen, people become ill and we have no control over weather-related disasters.

Your ability to manage an emergency situation depends on how well you prepare for those disastrous events. Preparedness for fires, break-ins, automobile accidents and robberies is not only a smart business practice, it is paramount to ensuring the overall safety of a business operation. Each establishment should have a safety plan in place and consider it an important segment of employee orientation. If you are unaware of your employer's safety plan, waste no more time—ask about it now.

---

### BECOME MORE COMFORTABLE WITH THE UNKNOWN
The following are good procedures to follow in order to lessen the risk
in the event of unforeseen situations.

- Take CPR and general first-aid courses
- Have a first-aid kit readily available
- Have emergency numbers visibly posted
- Know the location of all fire extinguishers
- Become trained on how to use a heart defibrillator
- Know the evacuation procedure in case of a fire
- Learn how to use a fire extinguisher
- Have flashlights available in case of a power outage
- Memorize accurate directions in the event emergency personnel must be called

---

Responding quickly but also staying calm and collected during times of injury or illness to others helps not only the victim, but reassures bystanders that the situation is being controlled in the best way possible. Being able to handle serious challenges in a professional manner will take your level of customer care to exceptional heights.

> "TO MY CUSTOMER: I MAY NOT HAVE THE ANSWER, BUT I'LL FIND IT. I MAY NOT HAVE THE TIME, BUT I'LL MAKE IT."
> ~ UNKNOWN

# DEVELOP QUALITY TELEPHONE SKILLS

The moment you pick up a telephone, body language and visual perceptions disappear and your tone of voice becomes the dominant factor. Almost the entire message you project over the telephone is the result of your inflection, articulation, volume control and pacing. With this in mind, it gives new meaning to the old adage, "It's not always what you say, but how you say it."

Inflection is the wave-like movement of highs and lows in your pitch that conveys what you are verbalizing. In other words, it is the way you emphasize aspects of what you are communicating to make a conversation interesting. Articulation centers on the pronunciation of words. Both play a large role in how well you express yourself over the telephone.

Volume control and pacing are no different. Because high volume intimidates and provokes clients, speaking in a moderate voice is the norm for pleasant customer care. Low volumes can be very effective in certain circumstances, especially when a patron is troubled. The pacing of a conversation has a great deal to do with the momentum between you and the client. By controlling the pace, the customer is more likely to pay closer attention to what you are saying, placing emphasis on what you deem most important. Always be aware of the client's pace first, though. By listening closely, you will quickly hear the tempo that is being established.

Continue to recognize the areas that you are most proficient in on the topic of quality telephone skills. Assess yourself on many of the basics, such as the usage of vocabulary, greetings, holds, transfers, returning calls, voice mail and taking messages. Now, expand your skill set by putting into practice the following:

- Before stepping out, leave word where you are going and when you will return.

- Answer your telephone promptly, before the second or third ring.
- Make sure to speak directly into the telephone—clearly, naturally and pleasantly.
- Personalize your conversation by using the caller's name as often as you can.
- Offer assistance to the caller if the person requested is unavailable.
- If you must place the caller on hold, ask permission first. If it is necessary for the caller to be placed on hold longer than one minute, offer to return the call.
- When taking messages, write down all essential information, repeat it back to the customer and double-check spelling.
- Thank the person for calling and offer any other pleasantries.
- Return all calls in a prompt manner.

One additional thought: More often than not, a customer's first impression of you and your product or service is through a telephone call. With that in mind, don't ever forget the impact a simple smile can have on your conversation with a client. The difference this one expression can make is quite astonishing—even over the telephone.

> "PEOPLE WANT TO TALK TO A
> REAL, LIVE, RESPONSIVE PERSON
> WHO WILL LISTEN AND HELP
> THEM GET SATISFACTION."
> ~ THEO MICHELSON

# Juggle Clients Gracefully

Everyone knows that having more is better than not having enough, especially when it comes to customers. However, when your establishment is busy, clients in person or over the telephone can become quite impatient—rattling even the most professional salesperson.

Learning how to juggle customers gracefully allows you to maintain control of hectic situations. Begin by acknowledging customers individually and determining their needs. Let them know you are assisting another client, but that they are important to you and you will give optimal service as soon as possible. Respectfully asking patrons to be patient or asking them politely to wait is very different than putting them off or saying you are too busy to help. Never leave a customer just standing there or on hold.

Frequently check with waiting clients to let them know they haven't been forgotten. If necessary, turn them over to a colleague with an introduction that indicates your co-worker is more than qualified to assist. Thank the patrons for their patience and understanding.

A good practice to follow is to develop methods for handling different situations and adapt them as necessary. Consider each of the following common circumstances and construct your plan of action. You will be better prepared and less likely to become frazzled when juggling clients:

- How do you manage customers who tell you they will not wait?
- What should you do if a waiting customer starts to leave before you have a chance to return?
- How should you behave toward a client who interrupts you while finalizing another transaction and then demands your immediate attention?
- How do you determine who to help first when several people walk in simultaneously and you are the only available representative?

Treat all customers with equal importance and respect—remember, each and every client is a VIP.

> "QUALITY IN A SERVICE OR PRODUCT IS NOT WHAT YOU PUT INTO IT. IT IS WHAT THE CUSTOMER GETS OUT OF IT."
> ~ PETER DRUCKER

# CAREFULLY MANAGE YOUR ANGRY CUSTOMERS

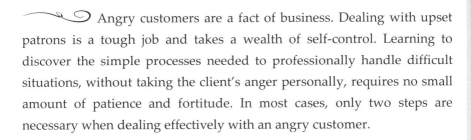
Angry customers are a fact of business. Dealing with upset patrons is a tough job and takes a wealth of self-control. Learning to discover the simple processes needed to professionally handle difficult situations, without taking the client's anger personally, requires no small amount of patience and fortitude. In most cases, only two steps are necessary when dealing effectively with an angry customer.

**Deal with the customer's FEELINGS first.** When confronted with a complaining patron, give the client your undivided attention. Ask questions to determine the problem, taking notes if necessary. Focus on the facts and describe the problem in your own words to be sure you understand and can empathize with how the customer feels.

**Deal with the customer's PROBLEM second.** No matter how unreasonable you think the patron might be, apologize for the inconvenience and perceived error. Explain the solutions you can offer, and ask the customer to choose an option. If that doesn't satisfy the client, ask what you can do to regain trust.

Take responsibility and personally resolve the problem if you can. If it is not within your capability, locate the appropriate person and explain that the problem needs immediate attention.

Remember—it's business, not personal. Put yourself in the client's shoes. How many times have you, as a patron, run into a litany of excuses when something went wrong? If you listen for understanding, apologize for the inconvenience, fix the problem and thank the customer for bringing the situation to your attention, you will increase the likelihood that the angry client will become your return customer.

> **IF YOU DON'T KNOW THE ANSWER, MAKE SURE TO ASK SOMEONE WHO DOES.**

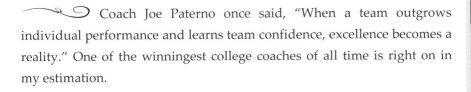

# WORK WELL WITHIN YOUR TEAM

Coach Joe Paterno once said, "When a team outgrows individual performance and learns team confidence, excellence becomes a reality." One of the winningest college coaches of all time is right on in my estimation.

Providing quality customer care takes teamwork. The power of individuals is most evident when working together as a team. Different team members give different perspectives and ideas toward positive customer relations.

A good team member understands how actions, tone and attitude affect the performance and success of co-workers. Good, respectful communication skills are the building blocks of a strong team as well. Those individuals who prefer to "go it alone" often struggle harder with less favorable results than those who rely on their surrounding team for support, direction and encouragement.

As team members, you are customers to one another. If you are at odds internally, no one can effectively take care of external clients. When disagreements arise, you must try to realize they can lead to new ideas, motivate change, produce synergy and help establish identities. However, if they become too overwhelming, the well-being of the entire team is threatened and a negative climate with less cohesiveness becomes the norm.

We've all heard the phrase, "There is no 'I' in team." It is important to remember there is also no room for territorial behavior in an honest team effort. Everyone's success is dependent on individual commitment to the team.

When you are compelled to stretch your limits, learn new ideas and discover new truths about yourself, you are transformed and propelled toward a common vision of quality and success. This vision serves as the catalyst for personal growth and organizational excellence.

> "COMING TOGETHER IS A BEGINNING. KEEPING TOGETHER IS PROGRESS. WORKING TOGETHER IS SUCCESS."
> ~ HENRY FORD

# MOVE FROM MARGINAL TO MEMORABLE

In a society that is becoming seemingly much more impersonal, finding ways to connect on a more individual basis means the difference between marginal and memorable. Text messaging, automated operators and other forms of electronic correspondence often detach us from personal interaction with others. With this in mind, there is still one practical way of conveying your utmost respect and gratitude: a handwritten thank you note.

As basic and outdated as it may seem, taking time from your busy schedule to sit down and write a handwritten note can make all the difference—especially in today's e-mail savvy world. Not only does it emphasize politeness and appreciation, it demonstrates the level of esteem you have for the person to whom you are sending the correspondence.

Showing your appreciation for your customer's patronage by sending a note will put the finishing touch on a memorable transaction. In addition, a thank you note should always be written for meals, gifts and services received; however, don't feel limited to expressing gratitude alone. If you have not communicated with a family member, friend or client in quite some time, reach out through mailing a simple note, just to say hello. You'll be glad you did.

> "THERE'S A PLACE IN THE WORLD FOR ANY BUSINESS THAT TAKES CARE OF ITS CUSTOMERS—AFTER THE SALE."
> ~ HARVEY MACKAY

# THE ART OF REMEMBERING NAMES

⟶◞◠ It has often been said, "There is nothing sweeter to the human ear than hearing someone else call you by name."

When providing the highest standard of quality customer care, consistently addressing clients by their first or last name adds an unforgettable touch. Even though this sounds like a no-brainer, accomplishing this task takes a concerted effort.

In Dale Carnegie's classic book *How to Win Friends and Influence People*, remembering names and using them often in conversation is listed as one of the best ways to create and maintain lasting relationships. According to Mr. Carnegie, the average person is more interested in his or her own name than in all the other names on earth put together. "One of the simplest, most obvious and most important ways of gaining goodwill is by remembering names and making people feel important—yet how many of us do it?"

Through formal or informal introductions, names are normally first shared and then absorbed. However, the big question is, for how long? Being able to recall a person's name after your initial meeting takes your full and undivided attention. You must begin by first hearing the name distinctly. If you are introduced to someone and you are unable to comprehend the name plainly, ask for it to be repeated.

Once clearly understood, repeat the name out loud in a statement or question such as, "Art, it is very nice meeting you," or "How long have you worked for this particular firm, Art?" Repetition is one of the most valuable methods to use when wanting to remember names.

Another helpful practice is to make quick and easy associations. This can be done by linking the name of the person you just met with someone you already know or a familiar picture, place or thing. Those who use this

189

particular technique depend on imagery and the similarities in the sounds of word endings.

Continue increasing your desire to not only hear names, but remember them. In accomplishing this, you will help yourself professionally, increase your circle of friends and show that you are genuinely interested in others.

> "If you want to be creative in your company, your career, your life; all it takes is one step...the extra one."
> ~ Dale Dauten

I hope you have enjoyed the ideas shared within this book. Each segment was carefully crafted with you, the sales professional, in mind. If the thought of selling with confidence is new to you, then hopefully you are already seeing improvements as a result of reading this book. If you are a seasoned veteran, then many of the concepts presented are a simple reminder of what you already know. Either way, never quit striving to maximize your sales potential while helping others do the same.

If you are a good presenter, reach out to someone who is not. If providing quality customer care comes easily to you, exemplify your hospitable nature continuously. Be the one who never stops learning, enjoying and leading those who not only want to do more, but be more.

**Paul Vitale** has become one of America's most sought-out professional speakers and trainers. Since founding Vital Communications, Inc. in 1996, Paul has authored several books, developed a handful of curriculums, published the first in a series of CD recordings, and energized hundreds of thousands throughout America and around the globe. His dynamic speaking style enthralls audiences and leaves them wanting more. Paul's ability to encourage people to reach their full potential has been described by his audiences as extraordinary. His expertise in various areas such as sales, leadership and customer service keeps him in high demand with clients such as ESPN, the Minnesota Vikings, the United States Postal Service, Southwest Airlines, Dole Hong Kong, Ltd. and the United States Chamber of Commerce.

Paul is a native of Russellville, Arkansas and received his degree in Mass Communications and Journalism from the University of Central Arkansas. In his spare time, Paul enjoys volunteering with Big Brothers/Big Sisters, Arkansas Children's Hospital and the Cystic Fibrosis Foundation. He is a graduate of Leadership Greater Little Rock and was named one of the "40 under 40" by *Arkansas Business*. Paul currently resides in Little Rock with his wife, Jessica.

*The true measurement of unlocking my potential is how I employ the ideas discovered within this book and use them to energize my enthusiasm as a sales professional. With that in mind, the following bullet points highlight the manner in which I plan to put into practice the methods learned within these pages.*

➤ _____
_____
_____

➤ _____
_____
_____

➤ _____
_____
_____

➤ _____
_____
_____

➤ _____
_____
_____

*This commitment will be reviewed in thirty days. At that point, if not before, the items listed above will have been implemented. This is the promise that I am making to myself.*

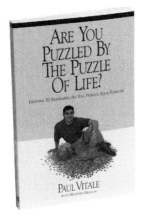

Paul's best seller, *Are You Puzzled by the Puzzle of Life?*, provides insight and encouragement into finding one's niche. With personal anecdotes and the contributing thoughts of successful people such as Bonnie Blair and George Clooney, Paul's book provides lessons for living, such as the importance of protecting one's reputation, taking personal and professional risks, and nurturing relationships. *Are You Puzzled by the Puzzle of Life?* is a vital tool for anyone who is searching for a purpose or is in pursuit of a dream.

ISBN 978-0-9666174-0-5
$15.00

*Pass It On* is a collection of inspirational and motivational quotes from a variety of individuals, past and present. With powerful and uplifting words from Dorothy Day, Martin Luther King Jr., George Bernard Shaw, John F. Kennedy and hundreds more, *Pass It On* gives voice to ideals for those eager to listen. You will discover 365 unique quotes that have been passed on from generation to generation. If you find pleasure in reading, collecting or teaching quotes to others, you can rely on *Pass It On* as a wonderful resource.

ISBN 978-0-9666174-2-9
$12.00

*Live Life Like You Mean It* is a theme that urges each of us to take full advantage of the time we have been allotted on this planet—no matter where we've been, where we are and where we plan to go. From start to finish, Paul encourages the listener to take action through the introduction of his five straightforward principles. It has been said, "Man reveals himself not in his thoughts, but in his actions." There is no better time than now to make a positive change, introduce an innovative idea, change your lifestyle or rebuild a relationship. No matter what it is….it's your life to live like you mean it.

ISBN 978-0-9666174-1-2
$15.00

*A Hero Within — Today's Youth, Tomorrow's Leaders* is a compelling curriculum intended to prepare students to succeed in this ever-changing world. From the classroom to the workplace, the lessons found in this program engage, challenge and encourage them to leave an everlasting mark. Each of the three independent units—**The Inner Workings of a Hero**, **Providing Heroic Customer Service** and **Presenting a Heroic Message**—contains a favorable amount of learning materials, interactive activities and resources designed to incorporate academic skills while engaging multiple intelligences throughout. This curriculum is not only an excellent coaching guide for STAR or other student organizations' competitive events, career and technical education classes as well as ELL students will find great benefit in the materials. If you are a teacher, administrator or counselor searching for an effective across-the-board program, *A Hero Within — Today's Youth, Tomorrow's Leaders* has been developed for you.

ISBN 978-0-9666174-3-6

*Call for information.*

## Also by Paul Vitale

*Are You Puzzled by the Puzzle of Life? Teacher's Guide*
*Dazzle Them With Customer Service Teacher's Guide*
*Professional Presentation Coaching Guide*

All titles may be purchased in bulk for educational, business, fund-raising or sales promotional use. For additional information on these products as well as Paul Vitale's seminars and presentations, please contact Vital Communications, Inc. at 501-868-8195 or online at www.paulvitale.com.

Do you have questions, comments or suggestions?
Please share them with Paul! Write to him at the following address:

Mr. Paul Vitale
Vital Communications, Inc.
Post Office Box 2042
Little Rock, Arkansas 72203